A–Z

of

EMBROIDERED MOTIFS

SEARCH PRESS

First published in Great Britain 2014

Search Press Limited
Wellwood, North Farm Road,
Tunbridge Wells, Kent TN2 3DR

First published in Australia by
CB Publications
© CB Publications

ISBN: 978-1-78221-167-9

The Publishers and author can
accept no responsibility for any
consequences arising from the
information, advice or instructions
given in this publication.

Suppliers
If you have difficulty in obtaining
any of the materials and equipment
mentioned in this book, then please
visit the Search Press website for
details of suppliers:
www.searchpress.com

Printed in China

Bullion or grub stitch – hardly names which are poetic or enticing. But this little stitch, shaped into rosy clusters and sprinkled on anything from baby clothes to gardening gloves, has lured thousands into picking up a needle and rediscovering the gentle art of embroidery.

Who stitched the first bullion rose? We will probably never know, but the bullion knot has been used in embroidery since at least the early eighteen hundreds where it featured extensively in Irish Mountmellick work.

And where does it get such a strange name? It has many alternatives, such as caterpillar, coil or grub knot, Porto Rico rose, round or worm stitch and post or roll stitch. The name bullion undoubtedly comes from the similarity in appearance of the stitch to metal purl or bullion. This fine gold or silver wire is shaped into tiny coils then cut and couched to fabric with long stitches. The technique can be seen on military dress uniforms and ecclesiastical embroideries.

Whatever the origins of the name or of the stitch, we should all be thankful to the creator of the bullion knot, for creating something that we all have so much fun with! Use this book as a starting point and who knows what you will achieve.

Contents

General information

4   Threads
6   Needles
7   Fabrics
7   Embroidery Hoops
8   Transferring Designs
9   Left handed Embroiderers
24   Little Words of Wisdom
116   Appendix (patterns)
126   Index
128   Acknowledgements

Step-by step instructions

10   Starting and Ending
11   Bullion Knot
12   Bullion Loop
13   Couching a Bullion Knot
14   Tapered Bullion Knot
15   Long Bullion Knot
16   Classic Bullion Rose
20   Susan O'Connor Rose
22   Rose with Padded Satin Stitch Centre
23   Bullion Bud on Button

Expert's articles

44   Jenny Brown
52   Beverley Sheldrick
66   Kris Richards
66   Ros Haq
76   Lesley Turpin-Delport
112   Susan O'Connor

The designs

26   How to use this section
27   Alphabet
28   Animals
40   Australian Animals
45   Christmas
53   Flowers
67   Food
77   Miscellaneous
88   Nursery
92   Roses
113   Transport

Threads

The range of threads suitable for bullion embroidery is enormous and continually growing.

Some threads are more easily handled than others and it is possible to use the very finest of threads right through to lightweight string. Threads and yarns which have a tendency to break easily, or do not have a smooth surface such as chenille and bouclé, will cause the most frustrations for the bullion embroiderer.

All threads have a twist. Wrapping in a clockwise direction tends to untwist the thread and results in smoother bullions. Wrapping in an anti-clockwise direction puts extra twist into the thread and makes the bullion knots tighter and sometimes rougher in appearance.

All threads can be adversely affected by direct light, especially sunlight. The colour can fade quickly so store your threads in light resistant containers. Ensure that finished pieces of work are kept out of direct sunlight.

The dyes in some threads can be very unstable, so they are an unsuitable choice for items which will require washing. Bright and dark coloured threads and overdyed threads are the most likely to cause problems. To ensure the threads you wish to use are colourfast, work a few stitches on a scrap of your selected fabric and launder this in the same way that you intend to launder the finished project.

Stranded cotton

These low sheen threads come in an amazing variety of colours and are easy to work with. You can vary the thickness of a bullion knot by altering the number of strands used – fewer strands create a finer knot.

When using more than one strand at a time, it is important to separate the strands and then put them back together. This is known as 'stripping' the thread.

Perlé cotton

This thread is generally available in four different weights, or thicknesses – nos. 3, 5, 8 and 12. The larger the number, the finer the thread.

Silk thread

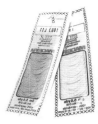

A wide range of silk threads, from flat untwisted filament silk to heavy twisted buttonhole thread, is available. Silk adds an extra lustre to bullion knots, which appeals to many embroiderers.

Crochet cotton

Crochet cottons are very strong and can be used to produce very even bullion knots. These low sheen threads are available in a wide variety of thicknesses.

Wool

Fine crewel wool is easy to work with and is available in many colours. For heavier stitches, tapestry wool can be used. Avoid 'fluffy' wool as the fibres tend to tangle when the thread is pulled through the wraps, making it difficult to form even stitches. Because of the natural 'spring' in wool and similar fibres, bullion knots are rarely as firm as those worked with other types of threads.

Rayon (viscose) thread

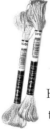

Rayon threads have a spectacular sheen, favoured by many embroiderers. However, they have a mind of their own and can be difficult to use.

There is a multitude of other synthetic threads which may be used for bullion embroidery.

Metallic thread

Metallic thread can be difficult to work with and can wear easily. Use short lengths of thread to make it more manageable.

Embroidery ribbon

Pure silk and rayon embroidery ribbon can be used for bullion embroidery. Despite efforts to keep the ribbon flat while working the wraps, the resulting knots are often roughly textured. This may be the effect you wish to achieve.

These identically worked bullion roses were made with different types of thread.

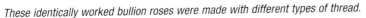

Tapestry wool   Persian yarn   Crewel wool   Stranded cotton   Stranded silk   Stranded rayon   No. 5 perlé cotton   Stranded metallic

Needles

Using a suitable needle makes a dramatic difference to the finished result.

The needle should easily pull through the wraps without distorting them. The eye and shaft must be of a consistent diameter. The needle should have a long even shaft and be the appropriate size for the thread you are using.

Straw (milliner's) needles

Straw needles, also known as milliner's needles, are ideal for bullion embroidery. They have a longer shaft than most needles and can accommodate a larger number of wraps.

The diameter of the shaft is consistent for almost the entire length of the needle, tapering off just before the point. The eye is only marginally wider than the shaft. This enables the wraps to be more uniform in size.

Sharps

These are a good general purpose needle. Because they have a small, round eye, they can be used for bullion embroidery. However, they do not have the length in the shaft to hold very many wraps.

Chenille needles

When working with wool or ribbon, chenille needles are the most suitable, despite the large eye. Wool is usually too thick to thread into a small-eyed needle such as a straw needle. Because wool is slightly elastic it has enough 'spring' to enable you to pull the needle through the wraps. It is important not to wrap the thread too tightly.

Yarn darners

Yarn darners are useful needles for thick threads and for working very long bullion knots. Again, it is important that the thread is not wrapped too tightly.

Crewel embroidery needles

These are unsuitable for creating beautiful bullion knots. The tapered shaft and large eye make them difficult to pull through without the wraps becoming distorted.

Straw needles	
Nos. 9–11	1–2 strands of stranded cotton, silk or rayon thread.
Nos. 5–8	3–4 strands of stranded cotton, silk or rayon thread.
Nos. 1–4	4–6 strands of stranded cotton, silk or rayon thread, no. 8 and no. 12 perlé cotton, coton á broder and metallic threads. Also suitable for Brazilian embroidery using thick, twisted threads.
Sharps	
Nos. 9–12	1–2 strands of stranded cotton, silk or rayon thread and other fine threads.
Nos. 7–8	2–3 strands of stranded cotton, silk or rayon thread.
Chenille needles	
Nos. 18–24	Embroidery ribbon, thick threads such as tapestry wool, crewel wool, no. 3 and no. 5 perlé cotton, thick silk and heavy metallic thread.
Yarn darners	
Nos. 14–18	Coarse threads and very long bullion knots.

No. 11 straw needle

No. 7 straw needle

No. 3 straw needle

No. 12 sharp needle

No. 7 sharp needle

No. 18 chenille needle

No. 24 chenille needle

No. 18 yarn darner

Fabrics & embroidery hoops

Fabrics

Almost any type of fabric is suitable for bullion embroidery, however it must be considered in relation to the thread being used. The weight and weave of the fabric will need to be able to support the weight of the stitches. Lightweight fabrics usually combine well with finer threads. Heavier threads are more suitable for thicker fabrics.

If using a stretch fabric, you may need to apply a fusible interfacing or similar, to the wrong side of the fabric to stabilise it before beginning the embroidery. Fur fabric may require a little trimming prior to stitching if the pile is very high.

Embroidery hoops

It is not advisable to use a hoop when working bullion knots. Because the needle is positioned in the fabric when working the wraps, it is easier to manipulate the thread, needle and fabric without the constraints of a hoop.

Embroidery hoops are a valuable aid when working 'stabbing' stitches where the needle passes to the front and back of the fabric in separate actions. The bullion knot is a 'scooping' stitch.

If you are combining other stitches that require you to stab the needle up and down, place the fabric in a hoop for these stitches. Remove it from the hoop to embroider the bullion knots.

Transferring the designs

Often bullion designs do not need to be transferred to the fabric you are embroidering.

Simple designs can often be worked freehand, bullion-by-bullion, until the motif is complete. More complex motifs may need to have some, if not all, of the design marked onto the fabric.

The colour and type of fabric you are using and the type of project, will largely determine the best method for transferring the design.

Fabric marking pens

These pens are non-permanent and are suitable for most light-coloured fabrics. They are not suitable for framed pieces as the ink may reappear. Lines made with spirit-based markers fade and disappear quickly.

Lines made with water-based markers are removed by dabbing or rinsing in cold water. Read the manufacturer's instructions carefully.

Transfer pencils

Transfer pencils are heat sensitive. Most leave permanent marks which need to be completely covered by the embroidery. Trace or draw a mirror image of the design onto white paper. Iron the design onto the right side of the fabric, using a 'press and lift' action with the iron.

Chalk-based fabric markers

These markers brush or wash off. They are excellent for dark fabrics but do tend to brush off quickly as the fabric is handled. Do not use on fabrics such as silk where water marks may be a problem. Draw or trace the design onto the right side of the fabric.

Lead pencils

Lead pencils can be used on light coloured fabrics and usually wash out. It is worth testing your particular fabric first as in some instances the marks are permanent. Mechanical pencils are particularly good for achieving fine, consistent lines.

Tacking

This is time consuming but leaves no permanent marks so the design can be altered as you progress. This method is excellent for wool blanketing or fabrics with a rough surface. Trace the design onto tracing paper, pin the tracing to the right side of the fabric. Using contrasting machine sewing thread and small stitches, tack along the lines of the design.

Score the tacked lines with the tip of a needle and tear the paper away. Remove the tacking as you embroider the design.

Note: avoid brightly coloured threads as these can shed tiny filaments onto your fabric.

Transfer papers

Dressmaker's carbon comes in several colours and is suitable for fabrics with a smooth surface. The chosen colour will need to show on the fabric but blend with the embroidery as the lines are permanent.

Place the carbon onto the fabric, waxed side down. Place the design over the carbon. Tape in place to prevent movement. Trace over the design lines using a sharp lead pencil or tracing wheel. Never use typewriter carbon paper.

Wax free transfer paper is available in several different colours and is used in exactly the same way as dressmaker's carbon. As it can be erased like pencil or rinsed out it is a very satisfactory method when working with smooth fabrics.

Left-handed embroiderers

If you wish to create smooth bullion knots, it is important to wrap the thread in a clockwise direction in the same manner as a right handed embroiderer would. Thread wrapped anti-clockwise puts in extra twist and makes the bullion tighter.

After placing the needle in the fabric, raise the tip of the needle with your right hand and wrap the thread with your left hand. As you pull the needle and thread through the wraps with your left hand, maintain tension on the thread with your right hand.

When working rounds of bullion knots, ie. for the petals of bullion roses, it is often easier to place the knots in an anti-clockwise direction. This will result in a rose that is a mirror image of one stitched by a right-handed embroiderer.

STARTING & ENDING

It is imperative when stitching bullion knots, as with other thread embroidery, to secure your thread at the beginning and end of your work. Each embroiderer has their own favourite way of starting and finishing, many using a knot. Because of the raised nature of bullion embroidery, a knot is quite acceptable. The following method will result in only a small dot on the front of the fabric which is covered by the first bullion knot.

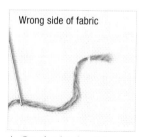

Wrong side of fabric

1 On the back, pick up approx. two fabric threads, taking a tiny 'scoop' stitch. Pull the thread through, leaving a 4mm (³⁄₁₆") tail.

2 Take a second back stitch into the same position but at right angles to the first stitch. Keep the thread under the tip of the needle.

3 Pull the thread through, pulling it towards you.

4 Pull the thread away from you to tighten.

5 Work a third back stitch into the same position on the fabric and in the same direction as the second stitch.

6 Pull the thread towards you and then away from you to tighten. You are now ready to begin your embroidery.

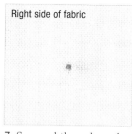

Right side of fabric

7 Secured thread on the right side of the fabric.

Ending off a thread

To end off a thread, work two tiny back stitches into your embroidery on the wrong side of the fabric. Run the thread under some of the embroidery for at least 6mm (¼") before trimming the thread. Where it is not possible to stitch into the back of the embroidery, work the back stitches into the wrong side of the fabric under the nearest bullion knot.

BULLION KNOT

The distance from A to B is the length of the finished bullion knot. To form a straight knot the number of wraps must cover this distance plus an extra 1–2 wraps.

1 Bring the needle to the front at A. Pull the thread through.

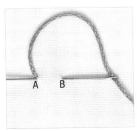

2 Take the needle to the back at B. Re-emerge at A, taking care not to split the thread. The thread is above the needle.

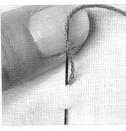

3 Rotate the fabric. Raise the point of the needle away from the fabric. Wrap the thread clockwise around the needle.

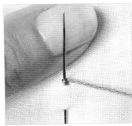

4 Keeping the point of the needle raised, pull the wrap firmly down onto the fabric.

5 Work the required number of wraps around the needle. Pack them down evenly as you wrap.

6 Keeping tension on the wraps with the left thumb, begin to ease the needle through the fabric and wraps.

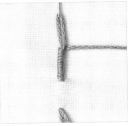

7 Continuing to keep tension on the wraps, pull the needle and thread through the wraps (thumb not shown).

8 Pull the thread all the way through, tugging it away from you until a small pleat forms in the fabric. This helps to ensure a tight even knot.

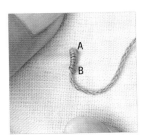

9 Release the thread. Smooth out the fabric and the knot will lay back towards B.

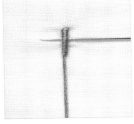

10 To ensure all wraps are even, stroke and manipulate them with the needle, maintaining tension on the thread.

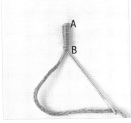

11 Take the needle to the back at B to anchor the knot.

12 Pull the thread through and end off. Completed bullion knot.

11

BULLION LOOP

A bullion loop is a variation of a bullion knot. It is formed in a similar manner, except that the distance between A and B is very short and the number of wraps is often large. Before anchoring the loop, take time to stroke and manipulate the wraps.

1 Bring the needle to the front at A. Pull the thread through.

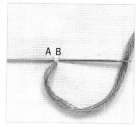

2 Take the needle through the fabric from B to A, taking care not to split the thread. The thread is below the needle.

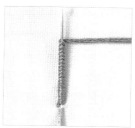

3 Rotate the fabric. Raise the point of the needle and wrap the thread around it following steps 3–5 for the bullion knot.

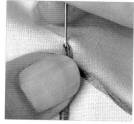

4 Holding the wraps firmly with your left thumb, begin to pull the needle and thread through the wraps.

5 Pull the thread all the way through. Using the needle, separate the wraps from the adjacent thread.

6 Hold wraps in place with your thumb (thumb not shown). Pull thread towards you to tighten wraps and curl them into a loop.

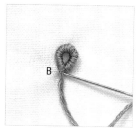

7 Take the needle to the back at B to anchor the loop.

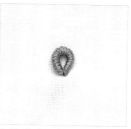

8 Pull the thread through. Completed bullion loop.

Bullion knots have been used in many forms of embroidery through the ages and have been known by various names. These include grub stitch, caterpillar stitch, coil stitch, knot stitch, post stitch, roll stitch, worm stitch and Porto Rico rose.

COUCHING A BULLION KNOT

Couching is used to hold long bullion knots in place, or to anchor a knot or loop into a particular shape. Use one strand of matching thread to ensure the stitches are invisible. Although we have shown a curved bullion knot here, the same method is used when couching a straight bullion knot.

1 Work the bullion knot. Roll it to the left hand side with your thumb. Bring the thread to the front beside the bullion knot.

2 Using the tip of the needle, separate the wraps of the knot next to where the couching thread emerged.

3 Take the couching thread over the knot. Insert the needle into the fabric very close to where it emerged.

4 Pull the thread through, manipulating it so it lies between the separated wraps.

5 Run your fingernail or needle over the wraps to hide the couching thread and ensure the wraps are even again.

6 Continue working couching stitches until the knot is anchored. Completed couched bullion knot.

An alternative method for couching, which is particularly useful when only 1–2 couching stitches are required, is to use the same thread you used for working the bullion knot. Place each couching stitch carefully so it appears as an extra wrap.

TAPERED BULLION KNOT

To form a straight bullion knot, the number of wraps must cover the distance from A to B. When forming a tapered bullion knot, the number of wraps is reduced.

1 Bring the needle to the front at A (this will be the 'blunt' end of the knot). Pull the thread through.

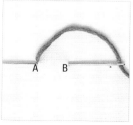

2 Take the needle to the back at B. Re-emerge at A, taking care not to split the thread. The thread is above the needle.

3 Rotate the fabric. Raise the point of the needle. Wrap the thread clockwise around the needle for the required number of wraps.

4 Keeping tension on the wraps with the left thumb, begin to ease the needle through the fabric and wraps (thumb not shown).

5 Continuing to keep ension on the wraps, pull the needle and thread through the wraps until a pleat forms in the fabric.

6 Smooth out the fabric. Give the knot an extra tug and let the wraps wind down at the end.

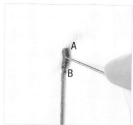

7 Using the point of your needle, push some of the wraps back towards A.

8 Hold the pushed back wraps and continue tugging to tighten the wraps on the lower segment to form a point (thumb not shown).

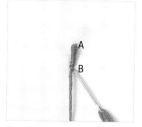

9 Take the needle to the back at B to anchor the knot.

10 Pull the thread through. Completed tapered bullion knot.

LONG BULLION KNOT

When working very long bullion knots, use the longest needle you can find, such as a straw (milliner's) needle, a long yarn darner or a doll needle.

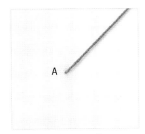

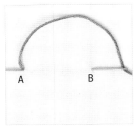

1 Bring the needle to the front at A. Pull the thread through.

2 Take the needle through the fabric from B to A, taking care not to split the thread. The thread is above the needle.

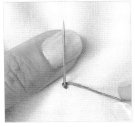

3 Rotate the fabric. Raise the point of the needle away from the fabric.

4 Wrap the thread around the needle in a clockwise direction.

5 Continue wrapping until the needle is almost full. Take care to keep the wraps even, and not to wrap too tightly.

6 Holding wraps at tip of needle, begin to pull thread through (fingers not shown). Stop when only a few wraps remain on the needle.

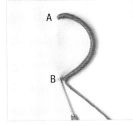

7 Continue wrapping the thread around the needle as before. Repeat steps 5–6 until the required number of wraps is achieved.

8 Firmly pull the needle and thread through the wraps. Pull the thread and manipulate the wraps until you are satisfied.

9 Take the needle to the back at B to anchor the knot.

10 Pull the thread through. Completed long bullion knot.

CLASSIC BULLION ROSE

This classic rose is created from two rounds of bullion knot petals surrounding a pair of bullion knots.

Indicates top of fabric

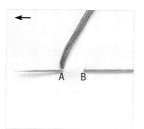

1 Centre. Using the darkest shade of thread, bring it to the front at A. Take the needle from B to A, taking care not to split the thread.

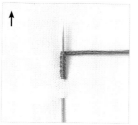

2 Rotate fabric so the needle points away from you. Raise the tip of the needle and wrap the thread clockwise around the needle six times.

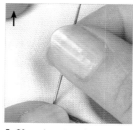

3 Keeping tension on the wraps with the left thumb, pull the thread through.

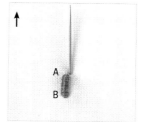

4 Anchor the bullion knot at B. Bring the needle to the front again, very close to A.

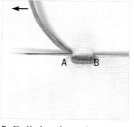

5 Pull the thread through. Rotate the fabric. Take the needle from B to A, keeping the thread above the needle.

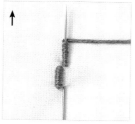

6 Rotate the fabric so the needle points away from you. Wrap the thread clockwise around the needle six times, holding the thread taut.

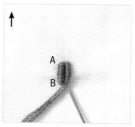

7 Take the needle to the back at B to anchor the second bullion knot.

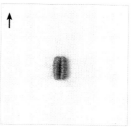

8 Pull the thread through and end off on the back of the fabric. Completed centre.

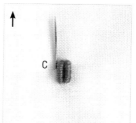

9 Inner petals. Change to a lighter shade of thread. Bring the needle to the front at C.

10 Take the needle from D to C, keeping the thread above the needle.

11 Rotate the fabric. Wrap the thread around the needle nine times. Pack the wraps evenly down the needle.

Roses of various sizes can be made by varying the thickness of the thread, number of strands and size of the needle. To form a particularly large rose, add more rounds of petals, increasing the number of wraps used in the knots in each subsequent round.

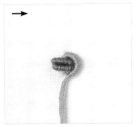

12 Pull the thread through, keeping it taut and settling the knot in position around the centre.

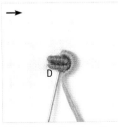

13 After adjusting the knot to your satisfaction, take the needle to the back at D to anchor the knot.

14 Completed first petal.

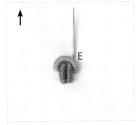

15 Rotate the fabric Bring the needle to the front at E.

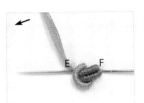

16 Pull the thread through Rotate the fabric slightly Take the needle from F to E.

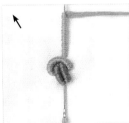

17 Rotate the fabric. Wrap the thread clock wise around the needle nine times, holding it taut to maintain tension on the wraps.

18 Pull the thread through. Settle the knot in position and adjust the wraps if necessary.

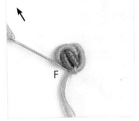

19 Take the needle to the back at F to anchor the knot.

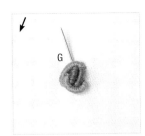

20 Pull the thread through. Rotate the fabric. Bring the needle to the front at G.

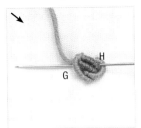

21 Pull the thread through. Rotate the fabric. Take the needle from H, inside the first petal, to G.

22 Rotate the fabric and wrap nine times. Pull thread through. Adjust the stitch. Take needle to the back at H, inside the first inner petal.

23 Pull through and end off the thread on the back. Completed inner petals.

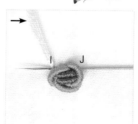

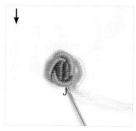

24 Outer petals. Rotate the fabric. Change to the lightest shade of thread. Bring the needle to the front at I.

25 Pull the thread through. Rotate the fabric. Take the needle from J to I.

26 Rotate the fabric and wrap the thread ten times. Form the stitch in the same manner as before. Take the needle to the back at J.

27 Pull the thread through. Completed first outer petal.

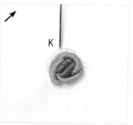

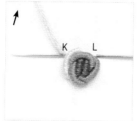

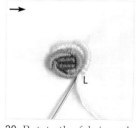

28 Rotate the fabric. Bring the needle to the front at K.

29 Rotate the fabric slightly. Take the needle from L to K.

30 Rotate the fabric and wrap the thread ten times. Form the stitch in the same manner as before. Take the needle to the back at L.

31 Pull the thread through. Completed second outer petal.

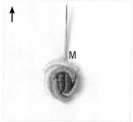

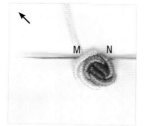

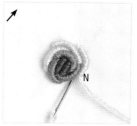

32 Rotate the fabric. Bring the needle to the front at M.

33 Rotate the fabric. Take the needle from N to M.

34 Rotate and wrap the thread ten times. Form the stitch in the same manner as before. Take the needle to the back at N.

35 Pull the thread through. Completed third outer petal.

Bullion roses are most effective when several shades of thread are used. No matter what colours you select, always begin with the darkest shade in the centre and grade to the lightest shade at the outer edge.

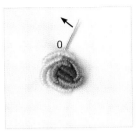

36 Rotate the fabric. Bring the needle to the front at O.

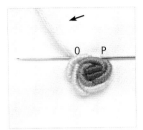

37 Rotate the fabric. Take the needle from P to O.

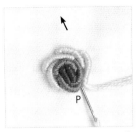

38 Rotate the fabric and wrap the thread ten times. Form the stitch in the same manner as before. Take the needle to the back at P.

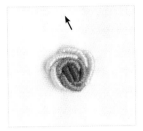

39 Pull the thread through. Completed fourth outer petal.

40 Rotate the fabric. Bring the needle to the front at Q.

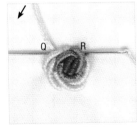

41 Rotate the fabric slightly. Take the needle from R to Q.

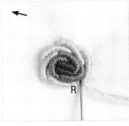

42 Rotate the fabric and wrap the thread ten times. Form the stitch in the same manner as before. Take the needle to the back at R.

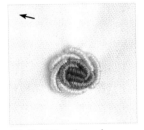

43 Pull the thread through. Completed fifth outer petal.

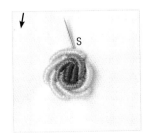

44 Rotate the fabric. Bring the needle to the front at S.

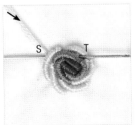

45 Rotate the fabric. Take the needle to the back at T (tucked inside the first outer petal). Re-emerge at S.

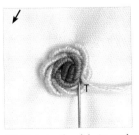

46 Rotate the fabric and wrap the thread ten times. Form the stitch in the same manner as before. Take the needle to the back at T.

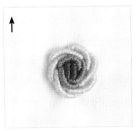

47 Pull the thread through and end off on the back of the fabric. Completed bullion rose.

THE SUSAN O'CONNOR ROSE

↑ Indicates top of fabric

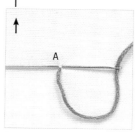

1 Centre. Begin with the darkest shade. Anchor thread and bring to front at A. Take a tiny stitch very close to A, leaving the needle in the fabric.

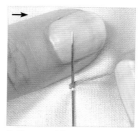

2 Rotate fabric so the needle faces upwards and away from you. Raise the tip of the needle off the fabric. Take the thread under the needle.

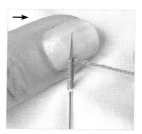

3 Wrap the thread evenly around the needle ten times in a clockwise direction. Ensure the wraps sit close together.

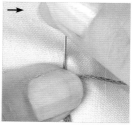

4 Placing your left thumb on the wraps to hold them firmly, begin to ease the eye of the needle through the wraps.

5 Pull the thread all the way through. Use the tip of the needle to separate the wraps from the adjacent thread.

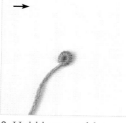

6 Hold loop on fabric with your left thumb and pull the thread firmly. Remove your thumb and release the tension on the thread.

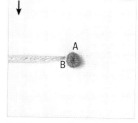

7 Take needle to back at A. End off. Inner petals. Rotate fabric. Change to medium shade. Bring needle to front at B, halfway along loop.

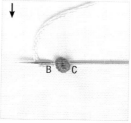

8 Take the needle from C to B, leaving it in the fabric.

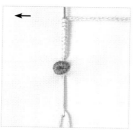

9 Rotate the fabric. Wrap the thread clockwise around the needle ten times.

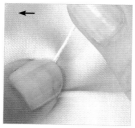

10 With your thumb over the wraps, pull the thread through the wraps. Pull tightly until the fabric forms a pleat.

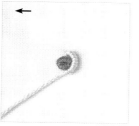

11 Release the tension on the working thread. Smooth out the fabric. This will cause the stitch to fall into position.

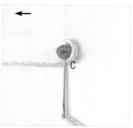

12 Take the needle to the back at C.

20

This variation of the classic bullion rose uses three shades of pink thread. The centre is formed with a bullion loop and each inner petal is a half circle.

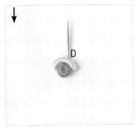

13 Pull the thread through. Rotate the fabric and re-emerge at D.

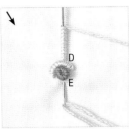

14 Rotate fabric. Take needle from E to D. Rotate so the needle points away from you. Wrap the thread around the needle ten times.

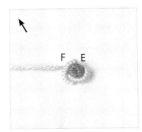

15 Pull thread through. Take the needle to the back at E to complete the second petal. Rotate the fabric. Bring the thread to the front at F.

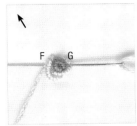

16 Take the needle from G (between the centre and first petal) to F.

17 Rotate so the needle points away from you. Wrap ten times and pull thread through. Take the needle to the back at G.

18 End off on the back. Outer petals. Rotate the fabric. Change to the lightest shade and bring the thread to the front at H.

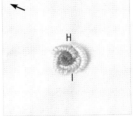

19 Rotate the fabric. Take the needle from I to H. Rotate and wrap the thread ten times. Complete the bullion knot as before.

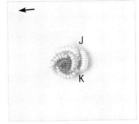

20 Rotate the fabric. Bring the needle to the front at J. Rotate and work a ten wrap bullion knot from K to J.

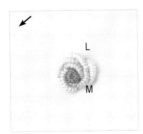

21 Rotate the fabric. Bring the needle to the front at L. Rotate and work a ten wrap bullion knot from M to L.

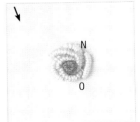

22 Rotate the fabric. Bring the needle to the front at N. Rotate and work a ten wrap bullion knot from O to N.

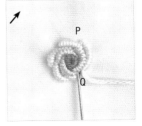

23 Rotate the fabric. Bring needle to front at P. Rotate and work a ten wrap bullion knot from Q to P. Q is just inside the first bullion knot of this round.

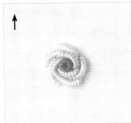

24 Pull the thread through and end off on the back of the fabric. Completed bullion rose.

ROSE WITH PADDED SATIN STITCH CENTRE

A square of padded satin stitch forms the centre of this rose. It looks particularly beautiful when stitched with 1–2 strands of silk thread.

↑ indicates top of fabric

1 Centre. Mark a small square with sides measuring approx. 6mm (¼") onto the fabric. Fill the square with vertical satin stitches.

2 Work a layer of horizontal satin stitches over the first layer.

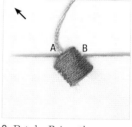

3 Petals. Bring the needle to the front at A, midway across the top of the square. Rotate the fabric. Take the needle from B to A.

4 Rotate fabric. Wrap thread around needle in a clockwise direction 8–10 times. The wraps touch each other but do not overlap.

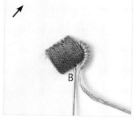

5 Pull the thread through the wraps. Take the needle to the back at B.

6 Pull the thread through. Completed first petal.

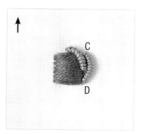

7 Rotate fabric. Bring needle to front at C approx. halfway along the first knot. Rotate fabric. Take needle from D to C. Rotate and work a second bullion knot.

8 Work five more bullion knots in the same manner, rotating the fabric slightly before working each one.

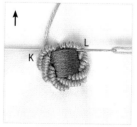

9 To work the last petal, rotate fabric and bring needle to front at K. Rotate and take it to the back at L, in between the first petal and the centre. Re-emerge at K.

10 Complete the bullion knot in the same manner as before. Completed rose with padded satin stitch centre.

BULLION BUD ON BUTTON

Bullion buds are a decorative way of attaching buttons. A four-holed button gives you more scope to be creative, but a delicate rosebud can be worked on a two-holed button.

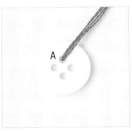

1 Position the button on the fabric so the holes form a diamond. Secure the thread on the back. Bring it to the front through upper hole (A).

2 Take the thread to the back of the fabric through the lower hole (B). Pull the thread firmly to anchor the button.

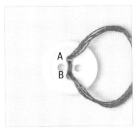

3 Inner petal. Re-emerge at A. Take needle to the back at B. Pull the thread through, leaving a large loop of thread on the front.

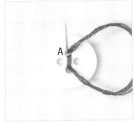

4 Re-emerge at A and leave the needle in the button. Hold the needle firmly on the back of the fabric with your left hand.

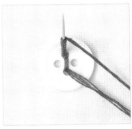

5 Wrap the loop of thread around the needle in a clockwise direction for the required number of wraps. Ensure they are evenly packed together.

6 Holding the wraps securely, carefully pull the thread through (thumb not shown).

7 Pull thread towards you until wraps are even and lie firmly against the button. Take the thread to the back at B and end off.

8 Outer petals. Change thread colour. Secure the thread on the back and emerge at A, just to the right of the inner petal.

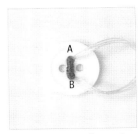

9 Take the needle to the back at B, just to the right of the inner petal. Pull the thread through leaving a large loop on the front as before.

10 Work the bullion knot in the same manner as the inner petal. Ensure it lies to the right of the inner petal.

11 Stitch a bullion knot on the left of the inner petal in the same manner to complete the bud.

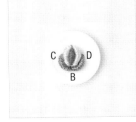

12 Leaves. Change thread colour. Work bullion knots from C to B and from D to B. End off the thread. Completed.

Little words of wisdom

Our panel of expert embroiderers answer the most commonly asked questions on bullions.

How many wraps should I use?

When wrapping the thread around the needle, push the wraps down onto the fabric so they are neat and compact. To work a straight bullion knot, the distance covered by the wraps on the needle should be the same as the length of fabric you have picked up with the needle. Add 1–2 wraps to this to eliminate the problem of the bullion knot looking 'ropey'. Adding more wraps will result in a curved bullion knot. When you can see the wraps as separate diagonal lines you do not have enough wraps on the needle.

The wraps are not even.

This is caused by uneven wrapping tension or by 'wrapping up' the needle rather than neatly packing the wraps down on one another as you wrap.

If the wraps are not even, lift the bullion knot up from the fabric and run the shaft of the needle under the wraps, pulling the thread at the same time. Don't be afraid to stroke and manipulate the wraps before anchoring the bullion knot.

A loop appears in the finished bullion knot.

Wrapping up the shaft of the needle, rather than keeping the wraps close together and close to the fabric, may cause large loops to form when the stitch is pulled through. Hold the knot on the fabric with your thumb and pull hard until the offending loop disappears.

The bullion knot is skinny at one end.

This is the result of too few wraps or the needle being too large for the thread. Rework the bullion knot using more wraps or a smaller needle.

The needle does not pull through the wraps.

This is usually due to the wraps being too tight around the needle or using an unsuitable needle, such as a crewel embroidery needle. Holding the needle and wraps between your thumb and forefinger, slightly twist the needle in the opposite direc-tion to the wraps. This will loosen the wraps.

Sometimes the thread will knot itself. This may happen if you pull the needle and thread through the wraps too quickly. Pull the thread back and untangle it, then pull the needle through slowly.

The fabric puckers.

The fabric may be too fine for the thread and amount of stitching you are applying to it. Begin again. You may be able to reinforce the fabric with interfacing or stabiliser depending on what your finished project will be.

Alternatively, you may be using too few wraps in your knots. Ensure the distance covered by the compacted wraps on the needle is the same as the length of fabric the needle has picked up, plus 1–2 wraps.

There is a straight thread running alongside the bullion knot.

The needle has been incorrectly positioned in the fabric when doing the wraps. The needle must enter the fabric away from the emerging thread and come to the front of the fabric just next to it.

The bullion knots do not lie flat.

If the bullion knots are placed too close together they will not have room to lie flat against the fabric. Give each knot sufficient room.

Marks appear on the fabric.

Some thread colours will shed tiny filaments onto the surrounding fabric. This can occur if the bullion knot is held hard against the fabric when the needle and thread are pulled through the wraps. Raise the needle off the fabric when pulling the thread through.

Why do my bulLion knots look different to someone else's?

Assuming the number of wraps is the same, the size of the needle and the number of strands used will make a considerable difference. Threads that have been stripped will give a different finish to those that have not. How firmly you wrap the thread around the needle will also make a difference.

How do I press bullion embroidery?

Place the embroidery face down on a well padded smooth surface, such as a thick folded flannelette sheet, and press lightly on the back. The normal padded surface of an ironing board does not offer enough padding.

My bullion embroidery has been pressed flat.

Lightly mist the bullion knots with clean water. Using a needle or your fingers, plump up the bullions by stroking and manipulating them until they have a more rounded shape. Press the fabric following the instructions previously given.

How to use this section

The following pages are filled with a vast array of delightful designs which incorporate bullion knots in their various forms.

For each design we have included various components which we hope will make it easy for you to glean the information or inspiration you require.

Pictorially each design is represented with a photograph, colour illustration and line drawing.

The colour illustration gives you an accurate picture of the stitches and their placement. Where appropriate small numbers have been included alongside some of the illustrations. These indicate the number of wraps to use for each individual bullion knot.

The line drawing (usually located beneath the title) shows the actual size of the design and is reproduced in the appendix for you to trace if you desire.

The text is made up of three parts. The beginning paragraphs for each design present you with a recom-mended order of work and additional useful information about creating the design.

The colour key lists the types and colours of threads or ribbons which are used to create the design. Many of the designs would look equally enchanting in alternative colour schemes, so we encourage you to experiment and modify these to suit your own needs and preferences.

The embroidery key provides you with information about the colour, stitch and number of strands used for each element of the design.

The number of wraps for knot stitches is also given. Because everyone's bullion knots are a little different, you will find that you may require slightly less or slightly more wraps to achieve the desired effect. The finish will depend on the needle used, thread chosen and tension applied.

For guidance in selecting an appropriate needle to use, refer to the needle chart on page 7.

Each piece of embroidery you stitch is unique and we hope this book helps you to fulfil your dreams.

Alphabet

Detailed instructions are given for the pictured monograms, however the entire alphabet is illustrated on page 116. For all letters, first work the bullion knots, couching them in place. The letters require tapered bullion knots where the bullions meet the narrower segments. Embroider these narrower segments in stem stitch. Add tiny flourishes at the end of letters with French knots where required.

Embroidery

A = A (3 strands, 3 bullion knots, 24–28 wraps; 1 strand, couching, stem stitch)
B = B (3 strands, 5 bullion knots, 12–30 wraps, French knot, 1 wrap; 1 strand, couching, stem stitch)
C = C (3 strands, 3 bullion knots, 12–25 wraps; 1 strand, couching, stem stitch)

Colour

DMC stranded cotton
A = 604 lt cranberry
B = 809 delft
Anchor stranded cotton
C = 260 lt pine green

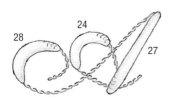

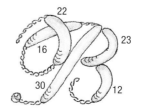

ANIMALS

Bee

This bullion-worked bee has padded satin stitch wings. To start, outline the thorax and abdomen in back stitch. Fill the thorax with satin stitch. At the top of the thorax, work two French knots for eyes. Starting at the tail end of the abdomen, work a black five-wrap bullion knot, beginning and ending just inside the outline. Alternating between the gold and black threads, stitch four bullion knots with seven wraps each. Place the knots side by side. Add a five-wrap gold bullion knot near the thorax to complete the abdomen.

Using the white thread, outline the wings in back stitch. Beginning at the thorax, fill each wing with long satin stitches for padding. Work a second layer of satin stitches at right angles to the first.

Finally, work the legs in back stitch.

Colour

DMC stranded cotton
A = blanc
B = 310 black
Madeira Decora stranded rayon
C = 1470 old gold

Embroidery

Body outline = B (1 strand, back stitch)
Thorax = B (1 strand, satin stitch)
Abdomen = B and C (1 strand, 6 bullion knots, 5–7 wraps)
Wing outlines = A (1 strand, back stitch)
Wings = A (1 strand, padded satin stitch) *Eyes* = B (1 strand, French knot, 2 wraps)
Legs = B (1 strand, back stitch)

Buzzing bees

Large bees

Work the body with seven bullion knots, alternating between the black and yellow threads. Stitch two French knots for the eyes and work four detached chains for the wings, two on each side.

Small bees

Work these bees with a black French knot in the middle and a single yellow French knot on each side. Work two detached chains for the wings.

Colour

DMC stranded cotton
A = 310 black
B = 444 dk lemon
Anchor stranded cotton
C = 130 delft blue

Embroidery

Large bees
Body = A and B (2 strands, 7 bullion knots, 5–12 wraps)
Eyes = A (2 strands, French knot, 3 wraps)
Wings = C (1 strand, detached chain)
Small bees
Body = A and B (4 strands, French knot, 1 wrap)
Wings = C (1 strand, detached chain)

ANIMALS

Beehive

To begin, form the beehive with a bullion knot across the top of the door, then stitch seven horizontal knots, to the top of the hive. Couch the long bullion knots in place. Working downwards stitch five knots on each side of the doorway. Embroider the door next. To create the bees, work five bullion knots alternating from yellow to black. Add two loose fly stitches to each bee for wings, tucking the ends of the stitches under the body. Embroider each antennae with a straight stitch and a French knot beside the tip.

Colour

DMC stranded cotton
A = 300 vy dk mahogany
B = 310 black
C = 435 vy lt brown
D = 519 vy lt wedgewood
E = 726 golden yellow

Embroidery

Hive
Hive = C
(3 strands, 18 bullion knots, 10–28 wraps; 1 strand, couching)
Door = A
(3 strands, 4 bullion knots, 10–12 wraps)

Bees *Body* = B and E
(3 strands, 5 bullion knots, 6–8 wraps)
Wings = D
(2 strands, fly stitch)
Antennae = B
(1 strand, straight stitch, French knot, 2 wraps)

Frogs

For each frog stitch the body followed by the head. Add red French knot eyes to the tips of the outer bullion knots on the head. Stitch two bullion knots for each leg. Vary the angle of the legs to give the frogs individual characters. Add three tiny straight stitches to each leg for the toes.

Colour

DMC stranded cotton
A = 347 vy dk salmon
B = 523 lt fern green

Embroidery

Small frog
Body = B (3 strands, 4 bullion knots, 10–12 wraps)
Head = B (3 strands, 4 bullion knots, 6–8 wraps)
Legs = B (3 strands, 2 bullion knots for each leg, 8–10 wraps)
Toes = B (3 strands, straight stitch)
Eyes = A (3 strands, French knot, 1 wrap)

Large frog
Body = B (3 strands, 4 bullion knots, 12–15 wraps)
Head = B (3 strands, 4 bullion knots, 8–10 wraps)
Legs = B (3 strands, 2 bullion knots for each leg, 10–12 wraps)
Toes = B (3 strands, straight stitch)
Eyes = A (3 strands, French knot, 1 wrap)

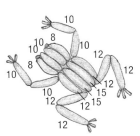

ANIMALS

Butterfly

Work the butterfly's body first, using a long bullion knot couched in place with matching thread. Start at the centre of each wing with a yellow bullion loop and work outwards. To allow the wings to be free, use one strand of blue thread and catch the bullions together on the underside with tiny running stitches. Do not take the stitches through the fabric. Alternatively, you may couch the bullion loops to the fabric. Work the antennae in pistil stitch.

Colour

DMC stranded cotton
A = 310 black
B = 335 rose
C = 725 dk golden yellow
D = 799 med delft
E = 986 dk forest green

Embroidery

Body = A (2 strands, bullion knot, 28 wraps; 1 strand, couching)
Upper wings = C (2 strands, bullion loop, 12 wraps), B (2 strands, bullion knot, 24 wraps), E (2 strands, bullion knot, 36 wraps), D (2 strands, bullion knot, 45 wraps)
Lower wings = C (2 strands, bullion loop, 8 wraps), B (2 strands, bullion knot, 20 wraps), E (2 strands, bullion knot, 25 wraps), D (2 strands, bullion knot, 30 wraps)
Antennae = A (1 strand, pistil stitch, 2 wraps)

Cat

Embroider the body of the cat using six vertical bullion knots, each with eighteen wraps. Stitch a sixteen-wrap bullion knot on each side.

Beginning at the neck, work three horizontal bullion knots for the head. Stitch an eighteen-wrap bullion knot on one side for the tail. Couch the tail in place, coaxing the knot into a gentle curve.

Work a tiny fly stitch for each ear. Add two straight stitches on each side of the head for whiskers.

Colour

DMC stranded cotton
A = 434 lt brown
B = 437 lt tan

Embroidery

Body = B (3 strands, 8 bullion knots, 16–18 wraps; 1 strand, couching)
Head = B (3 strands, 3 bullion knots, 10 wraps)
Tail = B (3 strands, bullion knot, 18 wraps; 1 strand, couching)
Ears = B (2 strands, fly stitch)
Whiskers = A (1 strand, straight stitch)

ANIMALS

Ducks

Work the first and second duck with three bullion knots for the body and two for the head. Add a French knot for the eye and a detached chain for the beak. For the diving

duck, work three bullions for the tail. Stitch the bullrushes with stem stitch and bullion knots. Embroider rows of stem stitch for the water and French knots for the splashes.

Colour

DMC stranded cotton
A = 370 med verdigris
B = 744 lt yellow
C = 809 delft

Embroidery

Paddling ducks
Body = B (2 strands, 3 bullion knots, 12–19 wraps)
Head = B (2 strands, 2 bullion knots, 7–9 wraps)
Eye = A (1 strand, French knot, 2 wraps)
Beak = A (1 strand, detached chain)

Diving duck
Tail = B (2 strands, 3 bullion knots, 9–14 wraps)
Bullrushes = A (1 strand, bullion knot, 9 wraps; 1 strand, stem stitch)

Water
Water = C (1 strand, stem stitch)
Splashes = C (1 strand, French knot, 2 wraps)

Robin red breast

Work the body of this delightful bird in bullion knots, starting from the stomach and working upwards. Follow the diagram as a guide for placement and thread colour, couching in position where necessary.

Embroider the worm with tiny back stitches. Work a fan of straight stitches to form the beak. Ensure the tip just covers a segment of the worm. Stitch the legs and feet with straight stitches.

Finish with a black French knot for the eye and an ecru straight stitch for the head marking.

Colour

DMC stranded cotton
A = ecru
B = 310 black
C = 436 tan
D = 666 bright Christmas red
E = 838 dk chocolate
F = 3371 black-brown

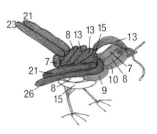

Embroidery

Bird
Stomach = A (2 strands, 2 bullion knots, 8–15 wraps)
Breast and face = D (2 strands, 4 bullion knots, 7–10 wraps)
Wing, head and back = E (2 strands, 10 bullion knots, 7–26 wraps)
Head marking = A (2 strands, straight stitch)
Beak = F (1 strand, straight stitch)
Legs and Feet = F (1 strand, straight stitch)
Eye = B (1 strand, French knot, 1 wrap)
Worm = C (1 strand, back stitch)

ANIMALS

Fishing frog

Paint the background and pond, using water colour pencils. Work the ribbon leaves first, then embroider the bullrushes. Work the reeds in a variety of green shades. Begin at the centre of each clump and work towards the sides. Stitch four bullion knots for the reeds lying on the bank.

Embroider the body of the fish next, alternating the colours of the bullion knots. Work the head and tail in satin stitch and outline the tail in straight stitch. Add straight stitches for the fins, fanning the stitches slightly. Work a colonial knot for the eye and a curved purple bullion knot for the remaining fin.

Next, work the fishing rod with two bullion knots and a long straight stitch. Stitch the line with one very loose straight stitch and one firm straight stitch. Work short straight stitches over the rod and line for the rod eyelet.

Embroider the frog starting at the head and working down the body. Work the frogs mouth over the face couching it at the centre.

Stitch each eye, beginning with a white French knot and surround this with a curved bullion knot. Add a second French knot on the white centre.

Position a twig just below the body of the frog. Stitch the front legs and upper sections of the back legs with bullion knots which go over the twig. Add the lower legs. Work a straight stitch, adding a French knot at the end, for each toe.

To finish, secure beads to the fabric for the water bubbles.

Colour

Anchor stranded cotton
A = 1 snow white
B = 99 dk lavender
C = 158 ultra lt teal
D = 169 dk teal
E = 240 vy lt Kelly green
F = 256 dk yellow-green
G = 257 vy dk yellow-green
H = 314 lt orange
I = 323 vy lt paprika
J = 376 vy lt mocha
K = 379 mocha
L = 875 lt blue-green
M = 879 ultra dk blue-green
N = 923 vy dk emerald
O = 1004 dk paprika
P = 1028 dk wine
Q = 1038 lt peacock blue
R = 1050 coffee brown
Mokuba no. 1540 embroidery ribbon
3.5mm (⅛") wide
S = 357 apple green
Mill Hill Glass Seed Beads
T = 02022 silver

ANIMALS

Embroidery

Reeds

Leaves = S (ribbon stitch)

Bullrushes = H and I (2 strands, stem stitch), R (3 strands, 2 bullion knots, 8 wraps)

Reeds = G (3–6 strands, bullion knot, 4–10 wraps), E, L and O (6 strands, bullion knot, 10–40 wraps)

Fish

Body = D and Q (3 strands, 23 bullion knots, 4–10 wraps)

Head = P (3 strands, satin stitch)

Eye = D (2 strands, colonial knot)

Fins = B (2 strands, straight stitch; 3 strands, bullion knot, 8 wraps)

Tail = B (3 strands, satin stitch, straight stitch)

Water bubbles = T (beading)

Fishing rod

Rod = K (3 strands, 2 bullion knots, 12 wraps), J (3 strands, straight stitch)

Line = C (4 strands, straight stitch)

Rod eyelet = J (3 strands, straight stitch)

Frog

Head = F (6 strands, 5 bullion knots, 7–9 wraps)

Body = F (6 strands, 5 bullion knots, 16 wraps)

Front legs = F (6 strands, 1 bullion knot for each leg, 16–24 wraps)

Back legs = F (6 strands, 2 bullion knots for each leg, 8–14 wraps)

Toes = F (4 strands, straight stitch, French knot, 2 wraps)

Mouth = M (3 strands, bullion knot, 20 wraps; 1 strand, couching)

Eye = A (4 strands, French knot, 2 wraps), M (1 strand, French knot, 3 wraps), N (2 strands, bullion knot, 16 wraps)

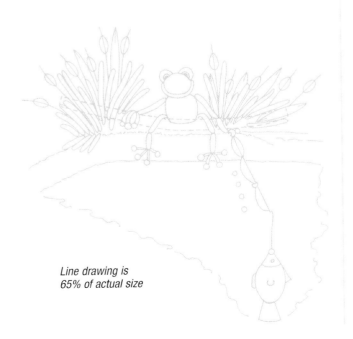

Line drawing is 65% of actual size

ANIMALS

Ladybirds and leaves

  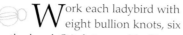 Work each ladybird with eight bullion knots, six for the body and two for the head. Stitch two red bullion knots side by side for the inner body. Add two bullion knots around the first pair for the outer body.

Using the black thread, work a six-wrap bullion between the inner and outer bullions on each side for the spots.

Embroider the head with two bullion knots. Work a six-wrap bullion knot just above the body, then a second bullion knot just above the first, curving it around the previous bullion.

For each leaf work two bullion knots, one along side the other, beginning and ending in the same holes. Work the second leaf in the same manner as the first, beginning at the base of the first leaf and angling the bullions of the second leaf to form a 'V' shape.

Colour

Anchor stranded cotton
A = 46 scarlet
B = 243 dk Kelly green
C = 403 black

Embroidery

Ladybird
Inner body = A (2 strands, 2 bullion knots, 12 wraps)
Outer body = A (2 strands, 2 bullion knots, 16 wraps)
Spots = C (2 strands, 2 bullion knots, 6 wraps)
Head = C (2 strands, 2 bullion knots, 6–10 wraps)
Leaves = B (2 strands, 2 bullion knots, 8 wraps)

Ladybird

 Embroider a long vertical bullion knot for the centre of the body. Starting from this knot and working outwards, stitch each wing with four bullion knots.

Beginning near the top of the wings, stitch three horizontal bullion knots for the head. Add the antennae and the legs with tiny straight stitches, taking the needle to the back of the fabric each time just under the bullion knots.

Colour

DMC stranded cotton
A = 310 black
Anchor stranded cotton
B = 46 scarlet

Embroidery

Centre of body = A (3 strands, 1 bullion knot, 16 wraps)
Wings = B (3 strands, 4 bullion knots for each wing, 10–14 wraps)
Head = A (3 strands, 3 bullion knots, 8 wraps)
Antennae = A (1 strand, straight stitch)
Legs = A (1 strand, straight stitch)

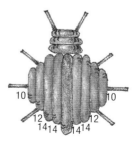

ANIMALS

Sheep 1

Begin the sheep by working vertical satin stitches for the face. Fill the body with bullion loops, beginning at the top and working downwards. Allow them to overlap each other. Stitch three vertical bullion knots for each leg. Work a single bullion knot for the tail and for each ear.

Colour

DMC stranded cotton

A = 310 black
B = 437 lt tan
C = 648 lt beaver grey

Embroidery

Face = B (3 strands, satin stitch)
Body = C (3 strands, 15 bullion loops, 16 wraps)
Ears = A (3 strands, 1 bullion knot for each ear, 8 wraps)
Legs = A (3 strands, 3 bullion knots for each leg, 8 wraps)
Tail = A (3 strands, bullion knot, 6 wraps)

Sheep 2

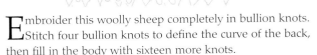

Embroider this woolly sheep completely in bullion knots. Stitch four bullion knots to define the curve of the back, then fill in the body with sixteen more knots.

To work the head, stitch a small centre bullion knot first, then place a longer bullion on each side. Add a bullion knot for the ear and a French knot for the eye. Work a single bullion knot for each leg.

Stitch the grass and stems with angled straight stitches and the flowers with French knots.

Colour

DMC stranded cotton

A = 310 black
B = 712 cream
C = 744 lt yellow
D = 798 dk delft
E = 3053 green-grey

Embroidery

Sheep
Body = B (3 strands, 20 bullion knots, 10–12 wraps)
Head = A (3 strands, 3 bullion knots, 7–11 wraps)
Ear = A (3 strands, bullion knot, 8 wraps)
Legs = A (3 strands, 1 bullion knot for each leg, 10 wraps)
Eye = D (3 strands, French knot, 1 wrap)
Grass and Flowers
Grass and stems = E (1 strand, straight stitch)
Flowers = C (2 strands, French knot, 1 wrap)

ANIMALS

Lion

Beginning with a bullion loop at the hind leg, work the body and hind leg first. Couch the knots in place. Stitch a bullion knot for each front leg and a shorter bullion knot for each paw.
　　Fill the face with vertical satin stitch. Stitch a French knot for each eye. Above each eye place a very small straight stitch for eyebrows. Work tiny satin stitches for the nose and two tiny fly stitches for the mouth.

To form the mane, surround the face with pale gold fly stitches which extend from the outer edge of the mane to the outer edge of the face. Using the yellow thread, work long straight stitches between the fly stitches. Randomly place small brown straight stitches at the tip of the mane and at the chin for contrast.

Work each ear with a detached chain. Stitch the tail in stem stitch. Add gold fly stitches and short overlapping brown straight stitches for the tail tip.

Colour

DMC stranded cotton
A = 436 tan
B = 676 lt old gold
C = 725 dk golden yellow
D = 838 dk chocolate

Embroidery

Body and back legs = A (2 strands, 7 bullion knots, 10–22 wraps; 1 strand, couching)
Front legs = A (2 strands, 2 bullion knots, 14 wraps)
Paws = A (2 strands, 1 bullion knot for each paw, 5 wraps)
Face = A (2 strands, satin stitch)
Eyes = D (1 strand, French knot, 2 wraps)

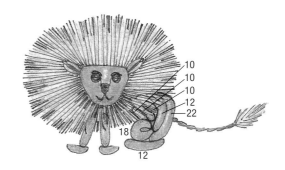

Eyebrows = D (1 strand, straight stitch)
Nose = D (1 strand, satin stitch)
Mouth = D (1 strand, fly stitch)
Mane = B (1 strand, fly stitch), C (1 strand, straight stitch)
Mane tips = D (1 strand, straight stitch)
Ears = A (1 strand, detached chain)
Tail = A (2 strands, stem stitch)
Tail tip = B (1 strand, fly stitch), D (1 strand, straight stitch)

ANIMALS

Poodles

For each poodle work the legs in bullion knots, eight knots for the grey dog and three knots for the black dog. Embroider the nose, neck and midsection of the body with satin stitch and the tail with stem stitch. Cover the front and rear body sections with tightly clustered French knots. Work the tip of the tail and the head in the same manner.

Work two bullion knots side by side for the ears and add a French knot for each eye. Embroider a horizontal detached chain for each paw.

Finally stitch three pink hearts between the dogs. Work two detached chains in a 'V' shape, anchoring each one in the same hole.

Colour

DMC stranded cotton
A = 310 black
Anchor stranded cotton
B = 25 vy lt carnation
C = 235 steel grey
D = 400 dk steel grey
Madeira stranded silk
E = 1802 steel grey
F = 1804 lt pearl grey

Embroidery

Grey poodle

Legs = C (2 strands, 8 bullion knots, 6–19 wraps)
Paws = C (2 strands, detached chain)
Body fur = E and F (2 strands, French knot, 1 wrap)
Body and neck = C (2 strands, satin stitch)
Head fur = E and F (2 strands, French knot, 1 wrap)
Nose = C (2 strands, satin stitch)
Ears = E (2 strands, 2 bullion knots, 9–10 wraps)
Eye = A (1 strand, French knot, 1 wrap)
Tail = C (2 strands, stem stitch)
Tip of tail = E and F (2 strands, French knot, 1 wrap)

Black poodle

Legs = D (2 strands, 3 bullion knots, 6–20 wraps)
Paw = D (2 strands, detached chain)
Body fur = A blended with E (1 strand of each, French knot, 1 wrap), A (2 strands, French knot, 1 wrap)
Body and neck = D (2 strands, satin stitch)
Head fur = A blended with E (1 strand of each, French knot, 1 wrap), A (2 strands, French knot, 1 wrap)
Nose = D (2 strands, satin stitch)
Ear = A blended with E (1 strand of each, 2 bullion knots, 7–8 wraps)
Eye = A (1 strand, French knot, 1 wrap)
Tail = D (2 strands, stem stitch)
Tip of tail = A (2 strands, French knot, 1 wrap), A blended with E (1 strand of each, French knot, 1 wrap)
Hearts = B (2 strands, detached chain)

37

ANIMALS

Squirrel

Begin with two bullion loops for the haunch, followed by two bullion knots along the squirrel's back. Fill in the remainder of the body with bullion knots. Couch the loops and knots in place with matching thread. Embroider three bullion knots for the head, two for the front legs and two to complete the back legs.

Add a tiny French knot for the nose and another for the eye. Work the ears with straight stitches.

Stitch the tail using several layers of randomly placed feather stitch, first working the orange-brown colour, then tan over the top. Scatter tiny black straight stitches along the tail for markings.

Stitch a single bullion knot for each acorn and work satin stitch across the top. Using blended threads, work the leaves with detached chains.

Colour

DMC stranded cotton

A = 300 vy dk mahogany
B = 301 med mahogany
C = 310 black
D = 433 med brown
E = 436 tan
F = 712 cream
G = 3347 med yellow-green

Embroidery

Squirrel

Haunches = A and B (2 strands, 2 bullion loops, 17–27 wraps; 1 strand, couching)
Back and body = A (2 strands, 4 bullion knots, 9–30 wraps; 1 strand, couching)
Front of body = F (2 strands, bullion knot, 14 wraps; 1 strand, couching)
Head = B (2 strands, 2 bullion knots, 11–24 wraps; 1 strand, couching)
Face = F (2 strands, bullion knot, 8 wraps)
Front legs = A and B (2 strands, 2 bullion knots, 11–16 wraps; 1 strand, couching)
Feet = A and B (2 strands, 2 bullion knots, 8–17 wraps; 1 strand, couching)
Eye and nose = C (1 strand, French knot, 2 wraps)
Ears = B (2 strands, straight stitch), F (1 strand, straight stitch)
Tail = B and E (1 strand, feather stitch)
Tail markings = C (1 strand, straight stitch)

Acorns

Nuts = D (2 strands, bullion knot, 5 wraps)
Top of nuts = E (2 strands, satin stitch)
Leaves = E blended with G (1 strand of each, detached chain)

ANIMALS

Mouse

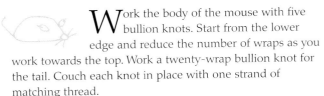

Work the body of the mouse with five bullion knots. Start from the lower edge and reduce the number of wraps as you work towards the top. Work a twenty-wrap bullion knot for the tail. Couch each knot in place with one strand of matching thread.

Add a detached chain for each ear and tiny satin stitches over the end of the longest bullion knot for the nose. Embroider four straight stitches at the end of the nose for whiskers.

Colour

DMC stranded cotton
A = 225 ultra lt shell pink
B = 310 black
C = 648 lt beaver grey

Embroidery

Body = C (3 strands, 5 bullion knots, 20–28 wraps; 1 strand, couching)
Tail = C (2 strands, bullion knot, 20 wraps; 1 strand, couching)
Left ear = C (2 strands, detached chain)
Right ear = A (2 strands, detached chain)
Nose = A (2 strands, satin stitch)
Whiskers = B (1 strand, straight stitch)

Rabbits

Embroider the body of each rabbit with four bullion knots, making the outer two bullions slightly longer than the inner two. Work a bullion knot for the tail.

Stitch three horizontal bullion knots for the head. Work the ears and whiskers in detached chain.

Scatter tiny green detached chains around the base of the rabbits for grass and leaves. Finish with pink French knot flowers.

Colour

DMC stranded cotton
A = blanc
B = 745 vy lt yellow
C = 778 vy lt antique mauve
D = 3013 lt khaki green
E = 3747 vy lt blue-violet

Embroidery

Rabbits
Body = C, B or E (2 strands, 4 bullion knots, 10–14 wraps)
Head = C, B or E (2 strands, 3 bullion knots, 8 wraps)
Ears = C, B or E (2 strands, detached chain)
Whiskers = C, B or E (1 strand, detached chain)
Tail = A (2 strands, bullion knot, 6 wraps)
Grass, flowers and leaves
Grass = D (1 strand, detached chain)
Flowers = C (1 strand, French knot, 2 wraps)
Leaves = D (1 strand, detached chain)

AUSTRALIAN ANIMALS

Koala

Stitch this favourite Australian animal, starting at the back and working towards the front. Couch the bullion knots in place. Stitch the haunch and head with a bullion loop at the centre and surround this with a curved bullion knot. Embroider the ears with fly stitch and straight stitch. Add French knots for the eyes and nose. Work the back paw with two fly stitches and the claws in straight stitch.

When you have completed the koala, work the tree trunk in small stem stitches and the leaves in detached chain.

Colour

DMC stranded cotton

A = ecru
B = 310 black
C = 451 dk shell grey
D = 840 med beige
E = 3364 pine green

Embroidery

Koala

Body and haunch = C (2 strands, 6 bullion knots, 8–30 wraps; 1 strand, couching)
Head = C (2 strands, 2 bullion loops, 11–26 wraps; 1 strand, couching)
Forelegs = C (2 strands, 2 bullion knots, 14–20 wraps; 1 strand, couching)
Ears = C (1 strand, fly stitch), A (1 strand, straight stitch)
Stomach = A (2 strands, bullion knot, 10 wraps)
Eyes = B (1 strand, French knot, 1 wrap)
Nose = B (1 strand, French knot, 4 wraps)
Back paw = C (2 strands, fly stitch)
Claws = B (1 strand, straight stitch)
Tree
Trunk = D (1 strand, stem stitch)
Leaves = E (1 strand, detached chain)

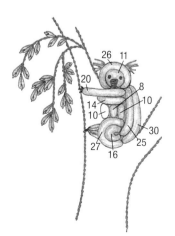

AUSTRALIAN ANIMALS

Kangaroos

Colour

DMC stranded cotton
A = 310 black
B = 451 dk shell grey
C = 632 vy dk mocha
D = 738 vy lt tan
E = 840 med beige
F = 3052 med green-grey
G = 3364 pine green
Anchor stranded cotton
H = 234 ultra lt steel grey

Embroidery

Standing kangaroo
Head = B (3 strands, 2 bullion knots, 7–8 wraps)
Back and tail = C (3 strands, 3 bullion knots, 27–35 wraps; 1 strand, couching)
Body = B (3 strands, 2 bullion knots, 9–17 wraps), H (3 strands, bullion knot, 27 wraps)
Haunch = B (3 strands, bullion loop, 25 wraps), H (3 strands, bullion knot, 32 wraps)
Hind legs = H (3 strands, 4 bullion knots, 10–15 wraps; 1 strand, couching)
Forelegs = B (3 strands, 2 bullion knots, 13–19 wraps)
Ears = B (3 strands, detached chain)
Eye = A (1 strand, French knot, 1 wrap)
Claws = A (1 strand, straight stitch)

Both kangaroos are stitched in a similar manner. Work the inner bullion loop of the haunch first. Working outwards from the loop, continue to fill the remainder of the haunch and the body with bullion knots. Couch the knots in position as you work.

Embroider two bullion knots for the head, then stitch the legs. The closest foreleg is worked over the top of the body to add dimension. Stitch the ears with detached chains and the claws on the feet and paws with straight stitches.

On the reclining kangaroo, work one straight stitch at the back of the head as illustrated.

Embroider the tree branches in stem stitch and the leaves in detached chain. Work the grass in fly stitch, alternating the colours.

AUSTRALIAN ANIMALS

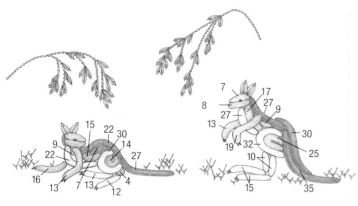

Echidnas

Beginning at the head of each echidna, fill in the body with bullion knots, working across the back and curving down towards the feet. Stitch the face in satin stitch and add a tiny French knot for the eye. Embroider a detached chain for each foot. Work the ants in tiny fly stitches.

Reclining

kangaroo *Head* = B (3 strands, 2 bullion knots, 7–8 wraps)
Back and tail = C (3 strands, 3 bullion knots, 7–27 wraps; 1 strand, couching)
Back of head = C (3 strands, straight stitch)
Body = B (3 strands, bullion knot, 15 wraps), H (3 strands, 2 bullion knots, 9–22 wraps)
Haunch = B (3 strands, bullion loop, 13 wraps), H (3 strands, bullion knot, 30 wraps)
Hind legs = H (3 strands, 3 bullion knots, 4–13 wraps; 1 strand, couching)
Forelegs = B (3 strands, 2 bullion knots, 13–16 wraps)
Ears = B (3 strands, detached chain)
Eye = A (1 strand, French knot, 1 wrap)
Claws = A (1 strand, straight stitch)

Trees

Branches = E (1 strand, stem stitch)
Leaves = G (1 strand, detached chain)
Grass = D and F (1 strand, fly stitch)

Colour

DMC stranded cotton

A = 301 med mahogany
B = 310 black
C = 838 dk chocolate

Embroidery

Echidna

Body = C (1 strand, 16–20 bullion knots, 15 wraps)
Head = B (2 strands, satin stitch)
Feet = B (2 strands, detached chain)
Eye = A (1 strand, French knot, 1 wrap)
Ants = B (1 strand, fly stitch)

AUSTRALIAN ANIMALS

Wombats

Begin the side view wombat at the head and work along the body, couching the bullions in place. Stitch the nose in straight stitch and the outer ears in detached chain. Work a straight stitch in the centre of each ear. Add French knots for the eyes. Work straight stitch shadows along the front of the legs.

Work the facing wombat and the rear view wombat in a similar manner. Begin with the central bullion loop and surround it with four bullion knots. Couch the knots in place. Add ears, nose and eyes in the same manner as those on the side view wombat. Work the feet on the facing wombat with blanket stitch. Stitch detached chain feet on the rear view wombat and add pink straight stitches to the middle of the left foot for paw pads.

Work the grass with tiny overlapping fly stitches and the dirt in straight stitch.

Colour

DMC stranded cotton
A = 310 black
B = 433 med brown
C = 760 salmon
D = 838 dk chocolate
E = 3052 med green-grey
Anchor stranded cotton
F = 382 black-brown

Embroidery

Side view wombat

Body and head = D (2 strands, 10 bullion knots, 11–30 wraps; 1 strand, couching)
Front legs = B (2 strands, 2 bullion knots, 10–11 wraps; 1 strand, couching)
Back legs = B (2 strands, 3 bullion knots, 14–22 wraps; 1 strand, couching)
Ears = D (2 strands, detached chain), C (2 strands, straight stitch)
Nose = C (2 strands, straight stitch)
Eye = A (1 strand, French knot, 2 wraps)
Claws = A (1 strand, straight stitch)
Shadows = D (2 strands, straight stitch)

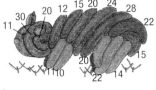

Facing wombat

Face = D (2 strands, 3 bullion knots, 18–30 wraps; 1 strand, couching)
Body = F (2 strands, 2 bullion knots, 27–45 wraps; 1 strand, couching)
Feet = D (2 strands, blanket stitch)
Ears = D (2 strands, detached chain), C (2 strands, straight stitch)
Nose = C (2 strands, straight stitch)
Eyes = A (1 strand, French knot, 2 wraps)

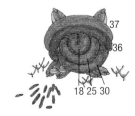

Rear view wombat

Body = D (2 strands, 4 bullion knots, 18–36 wraps; 1 strand, couching)
Top of back = B (2 strands, bullion knot, 37 wraps; 1 strand, couching)
Feet = D (2 strands, detached chain), C (2 strands, straight stitch)
Ears = D (2 strands, detached chain), C (2 strands, straight stitch)
Grass = E (1 strand, fly stitch)
Dirt = A (1 strand, straight stitch)

JENNY BROWN

I look at creating bullion motifs as a challenge. You are limited by the nature of the stitch and you must choose the number of wraps and position of the knots carefully, if you are to make the embroidery like the character you have in mind.

Animals are the motifs I most like to create. I enjoy capturing their character and how they look. For example, I had fun showing the wombat from the side, front and rear. I wanted to show his roundness as well as his little hind feet flinging dirt about. It was also interesting to stitch the kangaroo in his regal standing position, as well as his relaxed lounging pose.

Because I have a background in illustration, I generally begin with a drawing of the motif and usually find that if it is hard to draw, it will be difficult to stitch. I trace my final drawing onto the fabric with a water-soluble fabric marker. Then the fun begins, filling it in with bullion knots.

I use the direction and placement of the knots to help make the shape of the motif. For example, with animals like the kangaroo and squirrel, I usually start with a bullion loop for the back leg or haunch, followed by a long bullion knot for the shape of the back. I fill in the rest of the body and add a front leg over the other knots.

I like to keep a sense of humour when designing and stitching bullion motifs. For someone like me, who likes to work on a small scale, they are the perfect medium.

CHRISTMAS

Bells

Embroider these beautiful bells in bullion knots. Start with the inside of the bell, working one light brown bullion knot. Change to the gold thread and continue working bullion knots, decreasing in length to the top of the bell. Add a straight stitch line at the bottom of the bell in gold and a clapper embroidered in pistil stitch.

Work a bow with detached chain loops and back stitch ties embroidered over the bells. Stitch the bow knot in satin stitch.

Colour

Anchor stranded cotton
A = 133 dk royal blue
Madeira stranded silk
B = 2008 lt brown
C = 2209 med old gold

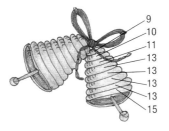

Embroidery

Bells
Inside of bell = B (2 strands, bullion knot, 14 wraps)
Outside of bell = C (2 strands, 8 bullion knots, 9–15 wraps; 2 strands, straight stitch)
Clapper = C (1 strand, pistil stitch, 2 wraps)
Bow
Loops = A (3 strands, detached chain)
Ties = A (3 strands, back stitch)
Knot = A (3 strands, satin stitch)

Bow

Work this two tone bow in bullion knots, couching the knots in position as you go. Embroider the outer bow loops, and then the inner ones using bullion loops. Add two bullion knots for each tie. Stitch the centre of the bow in satin stitch, ensuring it just covers the ends of the bullion knots.

Colour

DMC stranded cotton
A = 666 bright Christmas red
Madeira stranded silk
B = 0511 med garnet

Embroidery

Loops = A (3 strands, 2 bullion loops, 30–40 wraps; 1 strand, couching), B (2 strands, 2 bullion loops, 30–40 wraps; 1 strand, couching)
Ties = B (3 strands, 2 bullion knots, 24–27 wraps; 1 strand, couching), A (2 strands, 2 bullion knots, 30–33 wraps; 1 strand, couching)
Bow knot = A (3 strands, satin stitch)

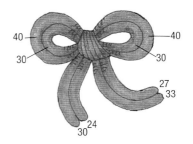

CHRISTMAS

Candles

Stitch these festive candles with long vertical bullion knots, couching the knots in position with a single strand of matching thread. Embroider the flames with two detached chains, one inside the other. Work the light haloes with little straight stitches. To finish, stitch the holly leaves in detached chain and the berries in French knots.

Colour

DMC stranded cotton
A = 725 dk golden yellow
Anchor stranded cotton
B = 133 dk royal blue
C = 304 dk pumpkin
Madeira stranded silk
D = 0511 med garnet
E = 1405 forest green

Embroidery

Candles
Candle = D (4 strands, bullion knot, 19 wraps; 1 strand, couching), B (6 strands, bullion knot, 15 wraps; 1 strand, couching)
Flame = A (2 strands, detached chain), C (1 strand, detached chain)
Light halo = A (1 strand, straight stitch)
Holly Leaves = E (1 strand, detached chain)
Berries = D (2 strands, French knot, 1 wrap)

Candy Canes

Work each candy cane with a single bullion knot. Starting at the curved end, couch the knots in position with one strand of matching thread. Embroider white straight stitch stripes diagonally over the bullion knots at approximately 3mm (⅛") intervals.

Colour

DMC stranded cotton
A = 666 bright Christmas red
Anchor Marlitt stranded rayon
B = 800 white

Embroidery

Cane = A (6 strands, bullion knot, 27 wraps; 1 strand, couching)
Stripes = B (2 strands, straight stitch)

CHRISTMAS

Christmas Pudding

Embroider the lower half of this plump Christmas pudding in horizontal bullion knots. Work vertical bullion knots for the brandy sauce.

Start at the base of the pudding and work upwards. Leave a space between the sixth and seventh bullion knots for a vertical knot. Work the brandy sauce from the outer edges inwards, slightly curving the bullion knots. Ensure one knot is tucked into the space previously left.

Embroider currants over the pudding using French knots. Add holly leaves in detached chain and berries in French knots.

Colour

DMC stranded cotton
A = 666 bright Christmas red
Madeira stranded silk
B = 1405 forest green
C = 1914 coffee brown
D = 2008 lt brown
E = 2207 vy lt old gold

Embroidery

Plum pudding = C (2 strands, 8 bullion knots, 5–22 wraps; 1 strand, couching)
Brandy sauce = E (2 strands, 9 bullion knots, 6–12 wraps; 1 strand, couching)
Currants = D (1 strand, French knot, 2 wraps)
Holly berries = A (2 strands, French knot, 2 wraps)
Holly leaves = B (1 strand, detached chain)

Holly

Work this versatile holly motif with bullion knots for the leaves and French knots for the berries. Stitch the centre of the leaf first, then add the sides. Embroider a cluster of three French knots for the berries.

Colour

DMC stranded cotton
A = 666 bright Christmas red
Madeira stranded silk
B = 1314 dk hunter green

Embroidery

Leaf centre = B (2 strands, bullion knot, 12 wraps)
Leaf sides = B (2 strands, 4 bullion knots, 5–6 wraps)
Berries = A (2 strands, French knot, 2 wraps)

CHRISTMAS

Christmas Tree 1

Work the trunk of this elegant Christmas tree in stem stitch.

Embroider the pot, beginning at the top and working horizontal bullion knots, decreasing the length of each bullion as you work down.

Stitch the branches of the tree with angled bullion knots, starting at the top on one side. Gradually increase the number of wraps in each knot as you work toward the pot. Repeat for the other side. Add a straight stitch star to the tip of the tree and straight stitch tinsel over the branches. Finish by couching the top bullion of the pot with metallic thread.

Colour

Anchor stranded cotton
A = 133 dk royal blue
Madeira stranded silk
B = 1405 forest green
C = 1914 coffee brown
Madeira metallic thread
D = 5014 black-gold

Embroidery

Trunk = C (1 strand, stem stitch)
Pot = A (3 strands, 4 bullion knots, 9–14 wraps)
Branches = B (2 strands, 12 bullion knots, 9–17 wraps)
Star and tinsel = D (1 strand, straight stitch)
Pot decoration = D (1 strand, couching)

Christmas Tree 2

Stitch this traditional Christmas tree in bullion knots, adding tiny red beads for decorations and a straight stitch star.

Embroider a single bullion knot for the trunk. Stitch the branches from the base to the tip following the illustration for the number of wraps in each bullion knot. The first bullion knot just covers the top of the trunk.

Work the star, taking each straight stitch from a point to the centre. Embroider three horizontal bullion knots for the pot. The upper knot just covers the lower end of the trunk. Attach eight beads for decorations.

Colour

DMC stranded cotton
A = 349 dk coral
B = 783 med topaz
C = 909 vy dk emerald green
Mill Hill antique seed beads
D = 03003 antique cranberry

Embroidery

Trunk = C (3 strands, 1 bullion knot, 8 wraps)
Branches = C (3 strands, 10 bullion knots, 6–24 wraps)
Pot = A (3 strands, 3 bullion knots, 8–12 wraps)
Star = B (1 strand, straight stitch)
Decorations = D (beading)

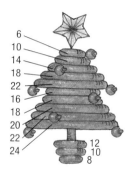

CHRISTMAS

Father Christmas

Colour

DMC stranded cotton
A = 124 variegated cornflower blue
B = 500 vy dk blue-green
C = 666 bright Christmas red
D = 909 vy dk emerald green
DMC no. 5 perlé cotton
E = blanc
DMC no. 8 perlé cotton
F = blanc **Anchor stranded cotton**
G = 1006 bright garnet

Embroidery

Father Christmas
Face = small piece of pink felt
Top of hat = C (6 strands, 6 bullion knots, 10–30 wraps)
Side of hat = C (6 strands, 6 bullion knots, 5–10 wraps)
Pompom = purchased white pompom
Eyebrows = E (2 strands, 2 bullion knots, 8 wraps)
Eyes = A (2 strands, colonial knot)
Mouth = G (1 strand, straight stitch)
Hair, beard and whiskers = E and F (1–2 strands, colonial knot, French knot, 1–2 wraps)
Holly
Berries = G (4 strands, French knot, 4–5 wraps)
Leaves = B and D (4 strands, 4–6 bullion knots, 4–6 wraps; 1 strand, couching; 3 strands, satin stitch)

Cut a circle of pink felt with a diameter of approximately 2.5cm (1"). Slip stitch in place. Work horizontal bullion knots for the hat, starting near the upper edge of the felt circle and working six knots to the top of the hat. Stitch six vertical bullion knots to form the side of the hat.

Embroider the eyebrows with bullion knots and the eyes with colonial knots. Work the mouth in straight stitch.

Lightly colour the cheeks with a red water colour pencil. Stitch the hair, beard and whiskers using a mixture of colonial and French knots.

Work 4-6 bullion knots to form the edges of the holly leaves, couching in place to form the shape. Fill the leaves with satin stitch. Embroider the berries in French knots.

To finish Father Christmas, stitch a pompom to the end of the hat. This may be purchased or you may choose to make one.

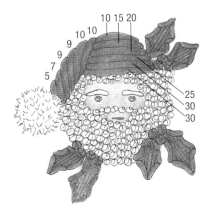

CHRISTMAS

Reindeer face

Embroider Rudolph the red nosed Reindeer in bullion knots, shaping the antlers by couching the knots into position with a single strand of matching thread. Work the longest segment first using a tapered bullion knot, then add the remaining segments. Embroider the nose and eyes with French knots and the mouth with a fly stitch.

Colour

Madeira stranded silk
A = 0511 med garnet
B = 1914 coffee brown
C = 2008 lt brown
D = 2400 black

Embroidery

Antlers = 2 strands of C blended with 1 strand of B (5 bullion knots for each antler, 7–17 wraps), B (1 strand, couching)
Nose = A (4 strands, French knot, 3 wraps)
Eyes = D (1 strand, French knot, 2 wraps)
Mouth = D (1 strand, fly stitch)

Wreath

Stitch this Christmas wreath with bullion knots, blending the green threads to give the variegated effect. Begin at the centre top and work two bullion knots in a 'V' shape as shown on the illustration. Working in an anti-clockwise direction, continue around the wreath, filling in with 'V's, until the wreath is complete.

Work tiny fly stitches around both edges of the wreath. Add red berries in French knots.

Finish with a bow, using two bullion loops and two bullion knots. Couch in place.

Colour

DMC stranded cotton
A = 580 dk moss green
B = 666 bright Christmas red
Madeira stranded silk
C = 1405 forest green

Embroidery

Wreath
Wreath = 2 strands of C blended with 1 strand of A (26 bullion knots, 6 wraps)
Edges = C (1 strand, fly stitch)
Berries = B (2 strands, French knot, 1 wrap)
Bow Loops = B (2 strands, 2 bullion loops, 30 wraps; 1 strand, couching)
Ties = B (2 strands, 2 bullion knots, 17 wraps; 1 strand, couching)

CHRISTMAS

Snowman

E mbroider this jolly snowman in bullion knots, starting at the base and working towards the top. Stitch the brim and then the top of the hat. Add the hatband with a single straight stitch. Embroider the nose with a tapered bullion knot and the eyes with French knots. Decorate the snowman with a back stitched scarf and French knot buttons. Add detached chain holly leaves and French knot berries to the base of the body.

Colour

DMC stranded cotton
A = 666 bright Christmas red
B = 970 lt pumpkin
Anchor Marlitt stranded rayon
C = 800 white
Madeira stranded silk
D = 1314 dk hunter green
E = 2209 med old gold
F = 2400 black

Embroidery

Snowman
Body and Head = C (2 strands, 12 bullion knots, 6–20 wraps)
Hat = F (2 strands, 4 bullion knots, 4–11 wraps)
Hatband = A (2 strands, straight stitch)
Nose = B (1 strand, bullion knot, 10 wraps)
Eyes = F (1 strand, French knot, 1 wrap)
Scarf = A (2 strands, back stitch)
Buttons = E (1 strand, French knot, 2 wraps)
Holly
Leaves = D (1 strand, detached chain)
Berries = A (2 strands, French knot, 2 wraps)

BEVERLEY SHELDRICK

When we think of bullion knots, we often think only of roses and rosebuds daintily enhancing a garment. However, they can be used in many other ways. I love to make starry little daisies using 6–8 bullion knots. Another lovely way to use them is as keepers for ribbon, especially on smocked baby garments and as narrow belt keepers.

When teaching a beginner, I like to start with wool. It is so much more forgiving than other threads. When pulling the wool through the wraps, it is easier to see exactly what is happening and how to stroke the wraps to get them sitting evenly before that final tug.

Once the bullion knot is mastered, pure silk thread is a wonderful medium. It performs beautifully, gives a lovely sheen, is easy to curve and manipulate, and makes such exquisite roses. Of course, the needle is absolutely crucial! A lovely long, straight needle, such as a straw needle, is essential.

To make tiny dainty roses, I work a triangle of three French knots very close together for the centre, rather than two bullion knots. This makes it easier to keep the roses round. When choosing colours for bullion roses, I am always surprised at the tonal jump required. For example, when purchasing stranded cottons remember you are seeing a greater intensity of colour in the skein than you will see when using 1–2 strands.

My favourite colours for bullion roses are *DMC* 963 and 819 in the pinks, *DMC* 340 for lavender, and a' screaming' green - *DMC* 906. This is one of those dreadful colours that one's eye automatically jumps over when choosing threads, but it does wonders for pinks if used in small quantities.

FLOWERS

Gumnut

Embroider the bullion loop at the tip of the gumnut first and couch in place. Add two French knots in the centre of the loop for seeds. Work a bullion knot, curving it around and partially covering the tip. Following the illustration, work five more bullion knots, allowing each one to slightly curve around the previous one. Couch each bullion knot in place.

Stitch the three stems from largest to smallest. Embroider the leaves with long satin stitches that extend from the base to the tip.

Colour

DMC stranded cotton
A = 300 vy dk mahogany
B = 320 med pistachio green
C = 434 lt brown
D = 801 dk coffee brown

Embroidery

Tip = A (3 strands, bullion loop, 18 wraps;
1 strand, couching)
Seeds = D (2 strands, French knot, 1 wrap)
Body of gumnut = C (3 strands, 6 bullion knots,
6–24 wraps; 1 strand, couching)
Stem = C (3 strands, stem stitch)
Leaves = B (3 strands, satin stitch)

Bottlebrush

Beginning at the base, work the green centre for the length of the flower. Add five detached chains at the top, angling them slightly from one side to the other. Embroider the stamens along each side of the centre, randomly varying the number of wraps from 20–30. Stitch tiny yellow French knots near the stamen tips for pollen. Work the stem in stem stitch. Embroider two long thin detached chains for the leaves.

Colour

DMC stranded cotton
A = 367 pistachio green
B = 433 med brown
C = 666 bright Christmas red
D = 743 yellow

Embroidery

Flower centre = A (3 strands, stem stitch)
Top of flower centre = A (3 strands, detached chain)
Stamens = C (1 strand, approx. 50 bullion knots,
20–30 wraps)
Pollen = D (1 strand, French knot, 1 wrap)
Stem = B (2 strands, stem stitch)
Leaves = A (3 strands, detached chain)

FLOWERS

Pink daisy

Stitch three horizontal bullion knots very close together for the centre. Each petal is three bullion knots. Imagining the circle is a clock face, stitch petals at 12 o'clock and 6 o'clock, then at 3 o'clock and 9 o'clock. Fill in the remaining spaces.

Surround each petal with a detached chain, anchoring the stitch at the petal tip. Stitch two detached chain leaves on each side.

Colour

DMC stranded cotton
A = 225 ultra lt shell pink
B = 966 baby green
C = 3354 lt dusky rose
D = 3688 med tea rose

Embroidery

Centre = A (2 strands, 3 bullion knots, 12 wraps)
Petals = C (2 strands, 3 bullion knots, 15 wraps)
Petal outlines = D (2 strands, detached chain)
Leaves = B (3 strands, detached chain)

Polyanthus

For each flower, work five bullion loops around the centre circle. Couch each loop in place at the outer edge. Using the darker yellow thread, work a straight stitch inside each bullion loop. Fill the centre with a single French knot. Embroider the leaves in blanket stitch, keeping the stitches very close together. Work the stems in stem stitch.

Colour

DMC stranded cotton
A = 725 dk golden yellow
B = 727 lt golden yellow
C = 3347 med yellow-green

Embroidery

Petals = B (1 strand, 5 bullion loops, 24 wraps; 1 strand, couching), A (2 strands, straight stitch)
Centres = A (2 strands, French knot, 1 wrap)
Leaves = C (1 strand, blanket stitch)
Stems = C (1 strand, stem stitch)

FLOWERS

Flower cart

The pre-painted rustic cart is filled with masses of delicate blooms. Complete one group of flowers before beginning the next.

Colour

DMC stranded cotton

A = blanc
B = 211 lt lavender
C = 223 lt shell pink
D = 224 vy lt shell pink
E = 225 ultra lt shell pink
F = 340 med blue-violet
G = 402 vy lt mahogany
H = 524 vy lt fern green
I = 642 dk beige-grey
J = 743 yellow
K = 745 vy lt yellow
L = 754 lt peach
M = 758 vy lt terra cotta
N = 776 vy lt rose
O = 819 lt baby pink
P = 948 vy lt peach
Q = 963 ultra lt dusky rose
R = 977 lt golden brown
S = 3012 med khaki green
T = 3013 lt khaki green
U = 3031 brown groundings
V = 3041 med antique violet
W = 3042 lt antique violet
X = 3051 dk green-grey
Y = 3052 med green-grey
Z = 3743 vy lt antique violet
AA = 3752 vy lt antique blue

Roses

Three groups of roses are embroidered in the cart. Pale peach roses fill the pot at the front and dusky pink roses are embroidered near the centre. A group of pale pink roses fill the space above the rear wheel.

Stitch two bullion knots for the centre of each rose and surround this with three bullion knots. For the larger roses, add 2–3 more bullion knots. Work two straight stitches beneath each rose for the sepals and then a single straight stitch for the stem. Randomly stitch tiny detached chains and straight stitches for the leaves.

Each bud is formed with two bullion knots worked side by side. Embroider a fly stitch with a long anchoring stitch around each bud to form the calyx and stem. Work tiny green French knot buds on the top of the pot.

Pale peach roses

Large roses
Centre = M (1 strand, 2 bullion knots, 6 wraps)
Inner petals = L (1 strand, 3 bullion knots, 9 wraps)
Outer petals = P (1 strand, 2–3 bullion knots, 11 wraps)
Sepals = S (1 strand, straight stitch

Small roses
Centre = M
(1 strand, 2 bullion knots, 6 wraps)
Outer petals = L
(1 strand, 3 bullion knots, 9 wraps)
Sepals = S (1 strand, straight stitch)

FLOWERS

Flower cart continued

Rosebuds

Petals = L, M and P (1 strand, 2 bullion knots, 6 wraps)
Calyx = S (1 strand, fly stitch)
Green buds = S (1 strand, French knot, 2 wraps)
Stems = S (1 strand, straight stitch)
Leaves = S (1 strand, detached chain, straight stitch)

Dusky pink roses

Large roses
Centre = C (1 strand, 2 bullion knots, 6 wraps)
Inner petals = D (1 strand, 3 bullion knots, 9 wraps)
Outer petals = E (1 strand, 2–3 bullion knots, 11 wraps)
Sepals = S (1 strand, straight stitch)
Small roses
Centre = C and D (1 strand, 2 bullion knots, 6 wraps)
Outer petals = D and E (1 strand, 3 bullion knots, 9 wraps)
Sepals = S (1 strand, straight stitch)
Rosebuds
Petals = C and D (1 strand,
2 bullion knots, 6 wraps)
Calyx = S and X (1 strand,
fly stitch)
Stems = S and X (1 strand,
straight stitch)
Leaves = S and X (1 strand,
detached chain, straight stitch)

Pale pink roses

Large roses ***Centre*** = N (1 strand, 2 bullion knots, 6 wraps)
Inner petals = Q (1 strand, 3 bullion knots, 9 wraps)
Outer petals = O (1 strand, 2–3 bullion knots, 11 wraps)
Sepals = S (1 strand, straight stitch)

Small roses

Centre = N and Q (1 strand, 2 bullion knots, 6 wraps) ***Outer petals*** = O and Q (1 strand, 3 bullion knots, 9 wraps)
Sepals = S (1 strand, straight stitch)

Rosebuds

Petals = N and Q (1 strand, 2 bullion knots, 6 wraps)
Calyx = S (1 strand, fly stitch)
Stems = S (1 strand, straight stitch)
Leaves = S (1 strand, detached chain, straight stitch)

White and yellow daisies

Embroider twelve white daisies above the group of peach roses. Stitch the bullion knot petals first, varying the number of wraps in each one. Work a single French knot for each centre. Use straight stitches for the stems and leaves. Embroider nine pale yellow daisies at the rear of the cart, stitching them in the same manner as the white daisies.
White daisies ***Centre*** = J (1 strand, French knot, 2 wraps)
Petals = A (1 strand, 3–7 bullion knots, 6–9 wraps)
Leaves and stems = T and X (1 strand, straight stitch)

FLOWERS

Yellow daisies

Centre = R (1 strand, French knot, 2 wraps)
Petals = K (1 strand, 3–7 bullion knots, 6–9 wraps)
Leaves and stems = T and X (1 strand, straight stitch)

Pot of lavender

Fill the painted pot near the front of the cart with sprigs of lavender. Work the French knot flowers then the straight stitch stems.
Flowers = F blended with H (1 strand of each, French knot, 2 wraps)
Stems = H and Y
(1 strand, straight stitch)
Clumps of dirt = I (1 strand, French knot, 2 wraps)

Forget-me-nots

Stitch four pale blue flowers just to the right of the pot. Work the petals, followed by the centres. Add tiny granitos (3–4 straight stitches worked into the same two holes) for the leaves.

Petals = AA (1 strand, granitos)
Centre = K (1 strand, French knot, 1 wrap)
Leaves = Y (1 strand, granitos)

Marigolds

Four golden marigolds are positioned near the forget-me-nots. For each flower, stitch the centre first. Add the five French knot petals, placing them close against the centre. Work the stems in straight stitch and the leaves using tiny detached chains and straight stitches.

Centre = U (1 strand, French knot, 2 wraps
Petals = G (1 strand, French knot, 2 wraps)
Stems and leaves = Y (1 strand, straight stitch detached chain)

Mauve and lemon hyacinths

Stitched with blended threads, the small group of mauve hyacinths peek from above the marigolds. Embroider the flowers, then add the stems and leaves.

The lemon hyacinths sit just above the mauve hyacinths. Work the flowers in the same manner. Add tiny detached chains for the leaves.

Mauve hyacinths

Flowers = B blended with F (1 strand of each, French knot, 1 wrap) **Stems and leaves** = Y (1 strand, straight stitch)

Lemon hyacinths

Flowers = K (1 strand, French knot, 2 wraps)
Leaves = S (1 strand, detached chain)

Line drawing is 75% of actual size

FLOWERS

Flower cart continued

Gypsophila

White French knots form the gypsophila blooms at the top of the design. Work long vertical straight stitches for the stems.

Flowers = A (1 strand, French knot, 2 wraps)
Stems = Y (1 strand, straight stitch)

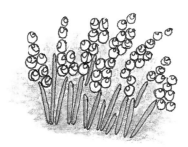

Lavender

A bunch of lavender is stitched to the right of the gypsophila. Work the bullion knot flowers with blended threads and the stems and leaves using fly stitch and straight stitch.

Flowers = F blended with H (1 strand of each, bullion knot, 5–7 wraps)
Stems and leaves = H (1 strand, fly stitch, straight stitch)

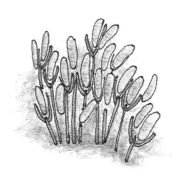

Wisteria

Five racemes of wisteria fill the rear of the cart. Begin at the top of each raceme and work downwards, changing the thread colour as you work. Embroider detached chain leaves at the top of the flowers and tiny straight stitch leaves along the sides.

Upper flowers = Z (1 strand, French knot, 2 wraps)
Middle flowers = W (1 strand, French knot, 2 wraps)
Lower flowers = V (1 strand, French knot, 2 wraps)
Leaves = Y (1 strand, straight stitch, detached chain)

Edging foliage

Long leafy fronds extend from each end of the cart. Embroider the stems in stem stitch and the leaves in detached chain.

Stems = H and Y (1 strand, stem stitch)
Leaves = H and Y (1 strand, detached chain)

FLOWERS

Foxglove

Embroider the stem first. To form the lower half of the plant, stitch clusters of three bullion knots for the larger flowers. Work the middle bullion knot first and then the outer knots, emerging very close to the top of the middle knot.

In the upper section of the plant, stitch two bullion knots very close together for each small flower. Add two French knots to the tip of the stem for buds.

Using green thread, embroider a fly stitch around the base of each flower. Finally, add three large detached chain leaves at the base of the plant.

Colour

DMC stranded cotton
A = 367 pistachio green
B = 760 salmon

Embroidery

Large flowers = B (3 strands, 3 bullion knots, 8 wraps)
Small flowers = B (3 strands, 2 bullion knots, 8 wraps)
Buds = B (3 strands, French knot, 1 wrap)
Stem = A (3 strands, stem stitch)
Sepals = A (3 strands, fly stitch)
Leaves = A (3 strands, detached chain)

Aster

Stitch the petals first, randomly varying the number of wraps in each one. Work tightly clustered French knots for the centre. Stitch the longer stem first, then the shorter one. Finally, work the leaf in satin stitch.

Colour

DMC stranded cotton
A = 367 pistachio green
B = 676 lt old gold
Anchor stranded cotton
C = 122 dk periwinkle blue

Embroidery

Petals = C (3 strands, approx. 19 bullion knots, 10–15 wraps)
Centre = B (3 strands, French knot, 1 wrap)
Stems = A (3 strands, stem stitch)
Leaf = A (3 strands, satin stitch)

FLOWERS

Sunflower

Embroider the petals first, stitching twenty-four bullion knots around the outer marked circle. Just inside the petals, work a circle of French knots using the dark green thread. Using the light green thread, work a second circle of French knots just inside the first. Fill the remaining space with black French knots. Work the stem in stem stitch and add two elongated fly stitches for the leaves.

Colour

DMC stranded cotton
A = 310 black
B = 320 med pistachio green
C = 367 pistachio green
D = 743 yellow

Embroidery

Petals = D (3 strands, 24 bullion knots, 10 wraps)
Centre = A, B and C (2 strands, French knot, 1 wrap)
Stem = C (2 strands, stem stitch)
Leaves = C (2 strands, fly stitch)

Hollyhock

Work the stem in stem stitch and the leaves in blanket stitch. Starting at the top of the spire, stitch small French knot buds. Embroider the uppermost bud with one wrap and the second bud with two wraps. Work the unopened flower immediately below using two bullion knots.

Stitch a bullion loop for each flower following the illustration. Couch the loops in place, ensuring they are round and overlap the leaves. Fill the centre of each bullion loop with tightly packed French knots.

Colour

DMC stranded cotton
A = 961 dk dusky rose
B = 3326 lt rose
C = 3363 med pine green

Embroidery

Flowers = A (3 strands, bullion loop, 15–40 wraps; 1 strand, couching),
B (2 strands, French knot, 1 wrap)
Unopened flower = A (3 strands, 2 bullion knots, 10 wraps)

Small buds = A (3 strands, French knot, 1–2 wraps)
Stem = C (2 strands, stem stitch)
Leaves = C (2 strands, blanket stitch)

FLOWERS

Lavender 1

Begin each flower at the tip and stitch towards the base, placing the bullion knots very close together. Work the stems down from the flowers.

For the ribbon, embroider four satin stitches across the stems and then work the flowing ties in stem stitch.

Colour

DMC stranded cotton
A = 554 lt violet
B = 676 lt old gold
Anchor stranded cotton
C = 121 periwinkle blue
D = 876 blue-green
Rajmahal art. silk
E = 45 baby camel

Embroidery

Lower flower heads = 2 strands of A blended with 1 strand of C (11 bullion knots, 6 wraps)
Upper flower heads = 2 strands of A blended with 1 strand of C (10 bullion knots, 6 wraps)
Stems = D (3 strands, stem stitch)
Ribbon around stems = E (1 strand, satin stitch)
Flowing ties = B blended with E (1 strand of each, stem stitch)

Lavender 2

Stitch nineteen bullion knots for the lavender flowers. Add the stems with straight stitch. Starting and finishing near the position for the bow knot, work a bullion loop for each bow loop. Beginning directly below the ends of the loops, stitch two bullion knots for the ties. Finally, add a bullion knot of four wraps for the bow knot.

Colour

DMC stranded cotton
A = 926 med grey-green
B = 3041 med antique violet
C = 3042 lt antique violet
DMC no. 5 perlé cotton
D = 778 vy lt antique mauve

Embroidery

Lavender
Flowers = 2 strands of B blended with 1 strand of C (19 bullion knots, 10 wraps)
Stems = A (1 strand, straight stitch)
Bow Loops = D (1 strand, 2 bullion loops, 25 wraps)
Ties = D (1 strand, 2 bullion knots, 18 wraps)
Knot = D (1 strand, bullion knot, 4 wraps)

FLOWERS

Pansy

Satin stitch the centre of the lower petal first. Starting and finishing near the top, work a bullion loop around the satin stitched centre. Couch in place. Work a second bullion loop around the first and couch in place. Form a third loop in the same manner.

Beginning from the centre and working outwards, work three bullion loops for the upper left petal. Work the upper right petal and then the upper centre petal in the same manner, couching all loops in place with matching thread.

Embroider a square of satin stitch at the centre of the flower. Add five straight stitches which extend from the centre over the satin stitching of the lower petal.

Stitch each leaf in satin stitch, completing one half before beginning the remaining half.

Colour

DMC stranded cotton
A = 310 black
B = 367 pistachio green
C = 676 lt old gold
Anchor stranded cotton
D = 870 lt antique violet
E = 871 antique violet
F = 873 vy dk antique violet

Embroidery

Centre of lower petal = C (3 strands, satin stitch)
Lower petal = D (3 strands, bullion loop, 20 wraps; 1 strand, couching), E (3 strands, bullion loop, 30 wraps; 1 strand, couching), F (3 strands, bullion loop, 40 wraps; 1 strand, couching)
Upper petals = D (3 strands, bullion loop, 15 wraps; 1 strand, couching), E (3 strands, bullion loop, 25 wraps; 1 strand, couching), F (3 strands, bullion loop, 35 wraps; 1 strand, couching)
Centre = A (1 strand, satin stitch)
Petal markings = A (1 strand, straight stitch)
Leaves = B (3 strands, satin stitch)

FLOWERS

Sunflowers

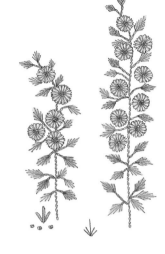

Colour

Anchor stranded cotton
A = 846 vy dk khaki green
Anchor Marlitt stranded rayon
B = 827 dk olive green
C = 869 topaz
D = 1011 lt olive green
E = 1077 butter yellow
Rajmahal art. silk
F = 29 charcoal

Embroidery

Sunflowers
Petals = C (1 strand, 12–15 bullion knots, 9–11 wraps)
Petal highlights = E (1 strand, straight stitch)
Centres = F (3 strands, French knot, 1 wrap)
Stems = A (2 strands, stem stitch)
Leaves = B and D (1 strand, straight stitch)
Grass
Small tuft = B (1 strand, straight stitch)

Large tuft = B blended with
D (1 strand of each,
straight stitch)
Knots = B blended with D
(1 strand of each,
French knot, 1 wrap)

S titch 12–15 bullion knots for the petals of each flower,
fanning them out from the centre marked circle. Fill the
centre with 4–6 tightly clustered French knots. Work a tiny
straight stitch between each petal for highlights.

Embroider the main stems in stem stitch. Work the leaves
in straight stitch, fanning the stitches out from the base.
Link each leaf to the main stem with tiny back stitches.

Stitch the tufts of grass with a fan of 3–5 straight stitches.
Add three French knots below the largest tuft of grass.

FLOWERS

Flannel flower

Form the eleven petals with pairs of bullion knots. When working the second bullion knot of each pair, tuck it under the tip of the first knot. Couch any wayward petals in place using one strand of thread. Fill the centre with tightly clustered French knots. Stitch a fly stitch around the tip of each petal with the anchoring stitch positioned exactly on the tip.

Colour

DMC stranded cotton

A = ecru
B = 613 lt taupe
C = 644 med beige-grey
D = 3047 lt yellow-beige

Embroidery

Petals = A (3 strands, 2 bullion knots for each petal, 15 wraps; 1 strand, couching)
Petal tips = D (2 strands, fly stitch)
Centre = B blended with C, and C blended with D (1 strand of each, French knot, 1 wrap)

Gum blossom

Stitch the cap first. Beginning with the longest bullion knot and working towards the shortest, work six bullion knots following the illustration. Embroider the stem in stem stitch. Work bullion knots for the stamens, randomly varying the number of wraps from 10–25. Begin each knot at the cap, fanning them out to form a loose semi - circle. Couch any long stamens in place with matching thread.

Embroider tiny French knots in and around the tips of the flower for pollen.

Colour

DMC stranded cotton

A = 602 med cranberry
B = 612 med taupe
C = 726 golden yellow

Embroidery

Stamens = A (3 strands, 15 bullion knots, 10–25 wraps; 1 strand, couching)
Pollen = C (2 strands, French knot, 1 wrap)
Cap = B (3 strands, 6 bullion knots, 4–14 wraps; 1 strand, couching)
Stem = B (2 strands, stem stitch)

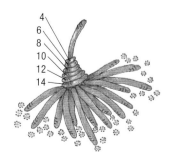

FLOWERS

Tulip

Embroider the inner petals in satin stitch. Starting at the base near the middle, work a pair of twenty-wrap bullion knots over the satin stitch for the centre outer petal.

Stitch two bullion knots on each side of the satin stitching for the remaining outer petals. For these petals, use twenty wraps for the knot closest to the satin stitching and twenty-five wraps for the outer knots.

Work the stem up to the flower in stem stitch. Using the same thread, work horizontal satin stitches for the calyx, just covering the top of the stem and the base of the flower. Finally, add the leaves using satin stitch.

Colour

DMC stranded cotton
A = 501 dk blue-green
Anchor stranded cotton
B = 46 scarlet
C = 47 dk Christmas red

Embroidery

Inner petals = C (3 strands, satin stitch)
Outer petals = B (3 strands, 6 bullion knots, 20–25 wraps; 1 strand, couching)
Calyx = A (3 strands, satin stitch)
Stem = A (3 strands, stem stitch)
Leaves = A (3 strands, satin stitch)

Wheat

Begin each wheat ear at the tip and stitch towards the base. Position the bullion knots very close together and alternate from one side to the other. Work the stems in stem stitch.

Form the ribbon by satin stitching across the stems. Embroider the flowing ribbons with stem stitch, adding a French knot at the ends.

Colour

DMC stranded cotton
A = 613 lt taupe
B = 3042 lt antique violet
C = 3046 med yellow-beige

Embroidery

Ears = A blended with C (1 strand of each, 11–14 bullion knots, 6 wraps)
Stems = A blended with C (1 strand of each, stem stitch)
Ribbon around stems = B (2 strands, satin stitch)
Flowing ribbons = B (2 strands, stem stitch)
Ribbon ends = B (2 strands, French knot, 1 wrap)

KRIS RICHARDS

I am quite passionate about roses, therefore bullion knots would be my favourite embroidery stitch. Most of my designs start with 2-3 bullion roses and flow from there.

I love to use soft pastel colours, my favourite colour combination being *DMC* pinks 223, 224 and 225. I use three colours to create depth in my roses and almost always use two strands of stranded cotton with either a no. 7 or no. 8 straw needle.

I have a basic order I follow when working roses, starting with two centre bullion knots of the darkest shade, then three bullion knots in the medium shade, and finally five outer bullion knots in the lightest shade. To create the effect of a garden filled with realistic roses, I stitch an uneven number of petals and usually make the roses touch each other to form a cluster before adding leaves, daisies and French knots to the design.

ROS HAQ

I find bullion knots fascinating. With bullions, it seems almost anything is possible.Nature provides lots of inspiration, but fantasy is just around the corner. Things my two grand-daughters enjoy, provide me with ideas and keep my stitching light-hearted and fun.

My bullion work, as with my other embroidery, seems quite large, but managing very long bullions is relatively easy. A long needle, such as a yarn darner, is important and I find not winding too tightly is essential. When the number of wraps outspaces the length of the needle, gently pull the needle through the fabric. Slide the wraps onto the thread and continue to add more wraps. A real bullion challenge would be a whole Noah's Ark and all the accompanying animals - maybe sometime in the future!

FOODS

Apples

W ork this delightful series of apples, starting with the whole apple and finishing with the core.

Embroider the first apple with vertical bullion knots working from the centre outwards. The two outer bullion knots on the right hand side are a blend of green and red threads.

Work the second apple in a similar manner to the first. However, with this apple, work three bullion knots on the right hand side using blended threads. Leave a gap on the left hand side for the bite. Fill in the apple flesh on the bite with satin stitch.

Embroider the third apple with just two bullion knots, couched into a circular shape. The right hand side bullion uses blended threads. Fill in the apple flesh with satin stitch and work tiny straight stitches for the seeds.

Stitch the final apple, or what's left of it, with two horizontal bullions for the skin and satin stitch for the apple flesh in between.

Work a bullion knot stalk at the top of each apple and two leaves in detached chain.

Colour

DMC stranded cotton
A = 666 bright Christmas red
B = 898 vy dk coffee brown
C = 3345 dk hunter green
D = 3347 med yellow-green
E = 3823 ultra lt yellow

 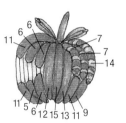

Embroidery

Skin = A (2 strands, bullion knots, 5–32 wraps), A blended with D (1 strand of each, bullion knots, 7–32 wraps)
Flesh = E (2 strands, satin stitch)
Seeds = B (1 strand, straight stitch)
Stalk = B (1 strand, bullion knot, 13 wraps)
Leaves = C (2 strands, detached chain)

FOODS

Beetroot

Embroider these beetroot with bullion knots, starting at the bottom and working upwards. Stitch three horizontal bullion knots. Change to the darker thread and work two more horizontal bullion knots.

Embroider the feathery tops with fly stitch and the stems with straight stitch.

Finish by working a line of back stitch for the vein of each leaf.

Colour

DMC stranded cotton
A = 814 vy dk garnet
B = 935 vy dk avocado green
C = 3685 wine

10
11
13
14
14

Embroidery

Lower section of beet = C (3 strands, 3 bullion knots, 13–14 wraps)
Upper section of beet = A (3 strands, 2 bullion knots, 10–11 wraps)
Stems = B (2 strands, straight stitch)
Leaves = B (2 strands, fly stitch)
Leaf veins = A (1 strand, back stitch)

Liquorice allsorts

These yummy sweets are deceptively easy to stitch. Each sweet has five horizontal bullion knots lying parallel to each other. To obtain a realistic shape, it is easier to begin by working the second and fourth bullions, leaving just enough space for one bullion in between. Then stitch the centre knot and the first and fifth bullion knots.

Colour

DMC stranded cotton
A = blanc
B = 310 black
C = 444 dk lemon
D = 603 cranberry
E = 703 lt Kelly green
F = 971 pumpkin

Embroidery

Centre layer = A and B (3 strands, bullion knot, 8 wraps)
Middle layers (2nd and 4th knots) = A and B (3 strands, bullion knots, 8 wraps)
Outer layers (1st and 5th knots) = A, B, C, D, E and F (3 strands, bullion knots, 8 wraps)

FOODS

Cabbages & cauliflowers

Thⁱs delightful vegie patch is embroidered almost entirely with bullion knots.

Starting with the centre of the cabbage, stitch four vertical bullion knots, two of each colour. Place the remaining bullion knots in a circular shape as shown in the illustration. Repeat for the remaining two cabbages.

Fill in the centres of the cauliflowers with cream bullion knots. Surround these knots with longer green bullion knots for the leaves. Start at the top left hand side and work around to the right hand side.

Colour

DMC stranded cotton
A = 712 cream
B = 3346 hunter green
C = 3363 med pine green
D = 3364 pine green

Embroidery

Cabbages
Dark green leaves = B (3 strands, 4 bullion knots, 10–14 wraps)
Light green leaves = D (3 strands, 8 bullion knots, 7–19 wraps)

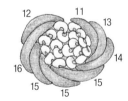
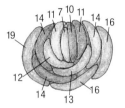

Cauliflowers
Centre = A (3 strands, bullion knots, 3 wraps)
Leaves = C (3 strands, 8 bullion knots, 11–16 wraps)

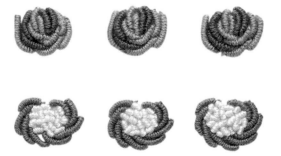

FOODS

Carrots in a basket

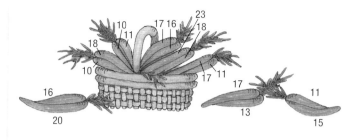

Work this bountiful basket of carrots in bullion knots, with the basket embroidered in woven filling stitch and the carrot tops in feather stitch.

Stitch the carrots in the basket first, using two bullion knots for each one. Start with the middle carrot and work outwards, leaving a space for the basket handle.

Stitch the carrots which have fallen out of the basket using tapered bullion knots.

Work the handle of the basket next, curving the top of the bullion knot and couching it in place. Stitch two horizontal bullion knots for the top of the basket, couching in position where necessary. Finish the basket handle with satin stitch between the bullion knot and the middle carrot.

Embroider the basket with woven filling stitch and the carrot tops with feather stitch. Overlap the feathery tops onto the basket and each other, as shown in the illustration.

Colour

DMC stranded cotton
A = 434 lt brown
B = 436 tan
C = 970 lt pumpkin
Anchor stranded cotton
D = 258 ultra dk yellow-green

Embroidery

Carrots
Carrots = C (2 strands, 16 bullion knots, 10–23 wraps)
Tops = D (1 strand, feather stitch)
Basket
Handle = B (2 strands, bullion knot, 22 wraps),
A (2 strands, satin stitch)
Rim = B (2 strands, 2 bullion knots,
35 wraps)
Body = B (2 strands, woven filling stitch)

FOODS

Fruits

Colour

DMC stranded cotton

A = blanc
B = 310 black
C = 307 lemon
D = 369 vy lt pistachio green
E = 500 vy dk blue-green
F = 520 dk fern green
G = 601 dk cranberry
H = 699 Christmas green
I = 712 cream
J = 816 garnet
K = 839 chocolate
L = 904 vy dk parrot green
M = 907 lt parrot green
N = 961 dk dusky rose
O = 3047 lt yellow-beige
P = 3078 vy lt golden yellow
Q = 3363 med pine green
R = 3803 lt wine

Anchor stranded cotton

S = 46 scarlet
T = 72 ultra dk wine
U = 100 vy dk lavender
V = 215 lt pistachio green
W = 240 vy lt Kelly green
X = 259 vy lt pine green
Y = 293 lt golden yellow
Z = 303 pumpkin
AA = 305 buttercup
BB = 316 orange
CC = 359 lt chocolate
DD = 376 vy lt mocha
EE = 683 ultra dk pistachio green

Mokuba no. 1540 embroidery ribbon 3.5mm (⅛") wide

FF = 357 apple green

This succulent collection of fruit is embroidered using a variety of stitches.

Pear

Work a vertical bullion knot for the core. Add two bullion knot seeds. Stitch the flesh in bullion knots, curving the knots around each seed. Stitch two outer bullion knots to form the skin and couch in place. Add a colonial knot to the base. Work the stem with a vertical bullion knot and each leaf with two bullion knots side by side.

Core = DD (1 strand, bullion knot, 15 wraps)
Seeds = K (1 strand, 2 bullion knots, 5 wraps)
Flesh = I (2 strands, 4 bullion knots, 12–20 wraps)
Skin = D (2 strands, 2 bullion knots, 30 wraps; 1 strand, couching)
Base = K (1 strand, colonial knot)
Stem = K (1 strand, bullion knot, 6 wraps)
Leaves = L (1 strand, 2 bullion knots, 8 wraps)

FOODS

Pineapple

Beginning at the top left of the fruit, embroider rows of bullion loops, stitching them close together. Work yellow colonial knots in the centre of the loops and partially surround each loop with a fly stitch.

Stitch seven dark green bullion knots from the top of the fruit. Work a light green bullion knot alongside each one. To finish, work a curved bullion knot, anchoring it on the upper section of the fruit.

Fruit = Q (1 strand, bullion loops, 25 wraps), C (1 strand, colonial knot), F (1 strand, fly stitch)
Top = EE (1 strand, 7 bullion knots, 10–15 wraps), V (2 strands, 8 bullion knots, 15–20 wraps)

Grapes

For the grapes, work overlapping bullion loops using two shades of purple thread. Work three green grapes in the same manner following the illustration for placement. Add white straight stitch highlights to several of the grapes near the centre of the bunch. Stitch the stalk with two bullion knots. To form the green tendril, wind the thread around a satay stick or skewer and spray with hair spray. Leave until dry. Carefully remove the curled thread from the stick or skewer. Work a loose straight stitch with the thread, maintaining the curled appearance.

Ripe grapes = T and U (2 strands, bullion loops, 8 wraps)
Green grapes = X (2 strands, 3 bullion loops, 8 wraps)
Grape highlights = A (1 strand, straight stitch)
Stalk = CC (1 strand, 2 bullion knots, 8–16 wraps)
Tendril = X (1 strand, straight stitch)

Banana

To create this banana, stitch two bullion knots side by side and then a shorter knot to form the lower end. Using brown thread, work a straight stitch directly below each long bullion knot and a French knot at the other end for the stalk.

Banana = AA (3 strands, 3 bullion knots, 5–17 wraps)
Markings = CC (1 strand, straight stitch)
Stalk = CC (1 strand, French knot, 4 wraps)

72

FOODS

Watermelon

Work four straight bullion knots for the flesh. Embroider three bullion knots for the rind, changing colour for each one and stitching from the centre towards the outer edge. Couch in place. Randomly scatter black straight stitches over the pink knots for the seeds.

Flesh = G (4 strands, 4 bullion knots, 15–25 wraps)
Rind = A (4 strands, bullion knot, 38 wraps;
1 strand, couching), W (4 strands, bullion knot, 43 wraps;
1 strand, couching), E (4 strands, bullion knot, 45 wraps;
1 strand, couching)
Seeds = B (1 strand, straight stitch)

Fig

First stitch the flesh, then the skin, stalk and base. Fill the centre with layers of randomly placed straight stitches, using the cream thread first, then the yellow and finally the pink.
Skin = E blended with T (1 strand of each, 2 bullion knots, 26 wraps), T (1 strand, couching)
Flesh = I (1 strand, 2 bullion knots, 20 wraps;
1 strand, couching)
Inner flesh = C, I and N (1 strand, straight stitch)
Stalk = T (1 strand, bullion knot, 8 wraps)
Base = T (1 strand, colonial knot)

Orange and lemon

The orange and lemon are both stitched in the same manner. Work two bullion loops, one inside the other, for the skin and rind. Beginning at the centre each time, fill the middle with bullion loops. Couch each one in place at the top of the loop.

Add a colonial knot to the centre. Stitch straight stitches over the middle bullion loops to define the segments of the fruit.

Embroider two bullion knots side by side for the dark green leaves. Work the light green leaves with ribbon stitch.

Orange
Skin = BB (2 strands, bullion loop, 40 wraps;
1 strand, couching)
Rind = A (2 strands, bullion loop, 36 wraps;
1 strand, couching)
Flesh = Z (1 strand, bullion loops, 25 wraps;
1 strand, couching)
Centre = A (1 strand, colonial knot)
Segment divisions = A (1 strand, straight stitch)

Lemon
Skin = Y (2 strands, bullion loop, 35 wraps; 1 strand, couching)
Rind = A (2 strands, bullion loop, 32 wraps; 1 strand, couching) *Flesh* = P (1 strand, bullion loops, 20 wraps; 1 strand, couching) *Centre* = A (1 strand, colonial knot)
Segment divisions = A (1 strand, straight stitch)

Leaves
Dark green leaves = H (2 strands, 2 bullion knots, 8 wraps)
Light green leaves = FF (ribbon stitch)

FOODS

Strawberries

Each of the three strawberries is stitched in the same manner. Fill the strawberry shapes with a cluster of tiny bullion loops. Randomly work yellow straight stitches over the knots for the seeds. Surround the lower half of the strawberry with a black fly stitch.
Form the leaves with 4–5 detached chains.

Berry = S (1 strand, 6–8 bullion loops, 8 wraps)
Seeds = AA (1 strand, straight stitch)
Outline = B (1 strand, fly stitch)
Leaves = L (1 strand, detached chain)

Apples

Embroider the red apple with a vertical bullion knot for the core. On each side of the core, work two bullion knots for the flesh and one for the seed. Embroider two curved bullion knots to form the skin of the red apple. Stitch the stem followed by the leaves. Work the body of the grub with a bullion knot and add French knots for the eyes.

Stitch the core, flesh, seeds and skin of the green apple in the same manner as the red apple, adding an extra cream bullion knot in the flesh on each side. Work a single bullion knot for the stem and a colonial knot at the base. Stitch the leaves in the same manner as the red apple.

Red apple
Skin = J (2 strands, 2 bullion knots, 25 wraps)
Core = DD (1 strand, bullion knot, 12 wraps)
Flesh = I (2 strands, 4 bullion knots, 14–20 wraps)

Seeds = K (1 strand, 2 bullion knots, 5 wraps)
Stem = K (1 strand, 2 bullion knots, 8 wraps)
Leaves = L (1 strand, 2 bullion knots, 8 wraps)
Grub
Body = W (1 strand, bullion knot, 10 wraps)
Eyes = K (1 strand, French knot, 1 wrap)
Green apple
Skin = M (2 strands, 2 bullion knots, 25 wraps)
Core = DD (1 strand, bullion knot, 12 wraps)
Flesh = I (2 strands, 6 bullion knots, 14–20 wraps)
Seeds = K (1 strand, 2 bullion knots, 5 wraps)
Stem = K (1 strand, bullion knot, 8 wraps)
Base = K (1 strand, colonial knot)
Leaves = L (1 strand, 2 bullion knots, 8 wraps)

Cherries

Work a bullion loop for the fruit of each large cherry and add straight stitches on one side of the loop for highlights. Embroider the stems with a single bullion knot each and then the leaves with two bullion knots side by side.

For each small cherry, work a bullion loop for the fruit and a bullion knot for the stem.

Large cherries
Cherries = R (2 strands, bullion loop, 14 wraps)
Highlights = A (2 strands, straight stitch)
Stems = O (1 strand, bullion knot, 12 wraps)
Leaves = E (1 strand, 2 bullion knots, 6 wraps)
Small cherries
Cherries = T (1 strand, bullion loop, 12 wraps)
Stems = AA (1 strand, bullion knot, 8–10 wraps)

FOODS

Peppers

Beginning at the base, work the plant stalk in stem stitch. Add a second line of stem stitch to the base, tapering it into the first line. Work each branch with a single line of stem stitch.

Work the three luscious peppers next. For each one work the centre vertical bullion knot first, then embroider a bullion knot on each side. Add a tiny straight stitch to the top of the red pepper to link it to the branch.

Embroider the leaves with long detached chains in clusters of two and three.

Colour

DMC stranded cotton
A = 349 dk coral
B = 500 vy dk blue-green
C = 743 yellow
D = 3346 hunter green
E = 3364 pine green

Embroidery

Stalk and branches = D (2 strands, stem stitch)
Yellow pepper = C (3 strands, 3 bullion knots, 9–12 wraps)
Red pepper = A (3 strands, 3 bullion knots, 8–11 wraps)
Stem on red pepper = D (1 strand, straight stitch)
Green pepper = B
(3 strands, 3 bullion knots, 9–12 wraps)
Leaves = E (2 strands, detached chain)

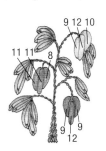

Radish

Embroider the bulb of this red radish with three bullion knots, working the centre knot first, then a slightly curved knot on each side to give the radish its round shape. Add the tail with back stitch.

Outline the leaves in back stitch and work the leaf veins in stem stitch.

Colour

DMC stranded cotton
A = 304 lt garnet
B = 3363 med pine green

Embroidery

Bulb = A (3 strands, 3 bullion knots, 6–8 wraps)
Tail = A (2 strands, back stitch)
Leaf outlines = B (1 strand, back stitch)
Leaf veins = B (1 strand, stem stitch)

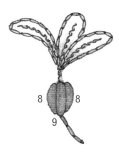

LESLEY TURPIN-DELPORT

My passion for this stitch is almost beyond description. It is without doubt the most versatile stitch I have ever used. A new embroidery student is initiated into my studio with 'Master the Bullion' as the first step into free-style embroidery. My aim is that they discover its potential and fall in love with this stitch.

The bullion is ideal for flower combinations, ranging from lavender and roses to daisies in many different interpretations. The mood and the flower will vary depending on the thread type, the number of wraps and the placing of the stitches. Lavender, for example, is created with a series of straight bullions, placed side by side, at an angle to the main stalk. The bulk of the bullion is achieved by selecting a no. 8 perle thread.

Roses are absolutely superb in bullion stitch. Tiny traditional rosebuds are delightful in stranded cotton, using one strand and changing colour with the darkest shade at the centre and finishing with a green bullion calyx on each side. The grub rose is simply stunning in variegated perle , beginning at the centre with elevated looped bullions surrounded by overlapping curved bullions.

The number of flower combinations which can be achieved with the bullion stitch is so vast that the embroiderer can have a lifetime of fun.

Having whet the appetite, one must remember to use a straw or milliner's needle for the perfect bullion. Do not be afraid to pull the drawstring firmly as this is the controlling thread of the bullion.

One little tip I would like to share with you - if the distance is too great for a bullion but you would like the stitch to resemble a bullion, use whipped stem stitch. It's ideal for tendrils or vine fronds.

MISCELLANEOUS

Boy 1

Colour

Madeira stranded silk
A = 0210 bright orange-red
B = 0306 lt peach flesh
C = 2004 black-brown
D = 2013 vy lt tan

Embroidery

Clothing = small pieces of fabric
Clothing outlines = A (1 strand, blanket stitch)
Arms and legs = B (2 strands, twisted chain stitch)
Hair = D (3 strands, straight stitch, bullion knots, 8–10 wraps)
Eyes = C (4 strands, French knot, 1 wrap)
Nose = C (1 strand, straight stitch)
Mouth = A (1 strand, back stitch)
Face outline = C (1 strand, back stitch)

To make this boy, cut out the shorts and shirt from two different fabrics. Back each piece with fusible appliqué paper. Appliqué the shorts to the background fabric using blanket stitch. Position the shirt so it just overlaps the top of the shorts and secure in the same manner.

Work the arms and legs in twisted chain stitch. Embroider the hair next, working a tangle of straight stitches for the fringe and bullion knots for the dreadlocks.

Add two French knots for the eyes and two angled straight stitches for the nose. Stitch the mouth and lower face outline in back stitch.

MISCELLANEOUS

Boy 2

Embroider this cute little boy with five horizontal bullion knots for the body of the overalls, followed by the legs and straps in vertical bullions. Stitch three scarlet knots between the straps for the shirt. Embroider the head from the chin upwards.

Stitch the arms and feet, keeping the bullion knots very close together. Finally, work five French knots for the hair.

Colour

DMC stranded cotton
A = 801 dk coffee brown
Anchor stranded cotton
B = 46 scarlet
C = 940 china blue

Embroidery

Body of overalls = C (3 strands, 5 bullion knots, 10 wraps)
Legs of overalls = C (3 strands, 2 bullion knots for each leg, 12 wraps)
Straps = C (3 strands, 1 bullion knot for each strap, 6 wraps)
Shirt = B (3 strands, 3 bullion knots, 6 wraps)
Head = A (3 strands, 6 bullion knots, 8–12 wraps)
Arms = A (3 strands, 2 bullion knots for each arm, 14 wraps)
Feet = A (3 strands, 2 bullion knots for each foot, 8 wraps)
Hair = A (3 strands, French knot, 2 wraps)

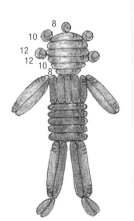

Girl

Start this little girl with the dress, working from the neck downwards. Couch the longer bullion knots in place using one strand of matching thread. Beginning at the neck, work six horizontal bullion knots upwards for the head. Work two bullion knots very close together to form each arm and leg.

Embroider nine pistil stitches fanned around the head for the hair. Add two French knot buttons to the upper section of the dress.

Colour

DMC stranded cotton
A = 602 med cranberry
B = 801 dk coffee brown
C = 992 aquamarine

Embroidery

Dress = A (3 strands, 9 bullion knots, 8–20 wraps; 1 strand, couching)
Head = B (3 strands, 6 bullion knots, 6–10 wraps)
Arms = B (3 strands, 2 bullion knots for each arm, 14 wraps)
Legs = B (3 strands, 2 bullion knots for each leg, 12 wraps)
Hair = B (2 strands, pistil stitch)
Buttons = C (2 strands, French knot, 2 wraps)

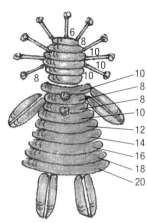

MISCELLANEOUS

Bathing huts

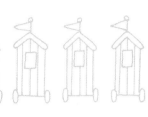

Embroider these colour-ful bathing huts with a variety of stitches. Begin with two bullion knots worked to form an inverted 'V' for the roof of the hut. Stitch five vertical rows of back stitch down from the roof.

Work the upper and lower edges of the windows with straight stitch and fill in between with satin stitch. Embroider each wheel with a bullion knot. Work a straight stitch flagpole on the top of each roof and finish with a French knot at the top. Stitch the coloured flags with two fly stitches, one inside the other.

Colour

DMC stranded cotton

A = ecru
B = 310 black
C = 321 vy lt garnet
D = 726 golden yellow
E = 986 dk forest green

Anchor stranded cotton

F = 142 bright blue

Embroidery

Red hut = C (2 strands, back stitch, 2 bullion knots, 13 wraps), D (2 strands, fly stitch)
Yellow hut = D (2 strands, back stitch, 2 bullion knots, 13 wraps), E (2 strands, fly stitch)
Blue hut = F (2 strands, back stitch, 2 bullion knots, 13 wraps), C (2 strands, fly stitch)
Green hut = E (2 strands, back stitch, 2 bullion knots, 13 wraps), F (2 strands, fly stitch)

Windows = B (2 strands, straight stitch, satin stitch)
Wheels = B (2 strands, 2 bullion knots, 8 wraps)
Flagpole = A (2 strands, straight stitch, French knot, 2 wraps)

MISCELLANEOUS

Bucket

Stitch the inside of this silvery bucket with tiny long and short stitches. Work the first row of stitches at the lower edge, using the darkest shade of grey. Change to the medium shade for the next row, then the lightest shade for the top row.

Embroider five vertical bullion knots just below the long and short stitch for the front of the bucket. Work a horizontal bullion knot for the rim and a second horizontal bullion knot for the base. Couch the rim in place near the centre. Finally, work the handle in stem stitch.

Colour

DMC stranded cotton
A = 645 vy dk beaver grey
B = 646 dk beaver grey
C = 647 med beaver grey
D = 648 lt beaver grey
DMC Art. 285 metallic thread
E = silver

Embroidery

Inside of bucket = A, B and C (2 strands long and short stitch)
Rim = 2 strands of D blended with 1 strand of E (bullion knot, 25 wraps), D (1 strand, couching)
Front of bucket = 2 strands of D blended with 1 strand of E (5 bullion knots, 16 wraps)
Base = 2 strands of D blended with 1 strand of E (bullion knot, 16 wraps)
Handle = 2 strands of D blended with 1 strand of E (stem stitch)

Feather

Work a long bullion knot for the quill and shaft. Couch into a gentle curve. Beginning near the top and stitching from side to side, work bullion knots along the shaft until 7mm (⁵/₁₆") from the end. Embroider the down at the base of the shaft in back stitch.

Colour

DMC stranded metallic thread
A = 5282 gold

Embroidery

Shaft = A (2 strands, bullion knot, 42 wraps, couching)
Feather = A (2 strands, 26 bullion knots, 8 wraps)
Down = A (1 strand, back stitch)

Watering can

Starting at the base, work seven horizontal bullion knots. Work a bullion knot for each handle and couch in place. Stitch a bullion knot for the neck of the spout and three for the rose.

Colour

DMC stranded cotton
A = 992 aquamarine

Embroidery

Can = A (3 strands, 7 bullion knots, 10–22 wraps)
Top handle = A (3 strands, bullion knot, 30 wraps; 1 strand, couching)
Side handle = A (3 strands, bullion knot, 25 wraps; 1 strand, couching)
Neck of spout = A (3 strands, bullion knot, 20 wraps)
Rose = A (3 strands, 3 bullion knots, 6–10 wraps)

MISCELLANEOUS

Clown with bouquet

Draw a circle 1cm (⅜") in diameter onto white felt. Work the facial features onto the felt. Cut out the face and secure it to the fabric with tiny blanket stitches. Working upwards, stitch three bullion knots for the hat. Embroider a cluster of French knots on each side of the face for the hair. Beginning at the centre and working outwards, stitch six vertical bullion knots for the shirt front and braces. Stitch the waistband next.

Stitch four bullion knots to create each trouser leg and sleeve. Embroider the two middle knots before working the outer ones. Working from the top downwards, stitch each boot. Add white French knots for pompoms. At the end of each sleeve, embroider three white straight stitches into the same holes for the hands. Stitching 3–5 French knots of each colour, embroider the flowers of the bouquet. Add four leaves to the top of the bouquet. For the stems, work three straight stitches above the hand and three below.

Colour

DMC stranded cotton

A = blanc
B = 310 black
C = 321 vy lt garnet
D = 335 rose
E = 792 dk cornflower blue
F = 971 pumpkin
G = 972 deep canary
H = 991 vy dk aquamarine

Embroidery

Head

Mouth = B (1 strand, fly stitch)
Nose = C (2 strands, French knot, 1 wrap)
Eyes = B (1 strand, fly stitch, French knot, 1 wrap)
Face outline = A (1 strand, blanket stitch)
Hair = F (4 strands, French knot, 1 wrap)

Hat

Brim = E (4 strands, bullion knot, 12 wraps)
Crown = E (4 strands, 2 bullion knots, 6–8 wraps)

Trousers

Braces = G (3 strands, 1 bullion knot for each strap, 12 wraps)
Waistband = G (3 strands, 2 bullion knots, 12 wraps)
Left leg = D and F (3 strands, 2 bullion knots, 22 wraps), E and G (3 strands, 2 bullion knots, 28 wraps)
Right leg = D and E (3 strands, 2 bullion knots, 22 wraps), F and H (3 strands, 2 bullion knots, 28 wraps)

Shirt

Front = C (3 strands, 4 bullion knots, 12 wraps)
Sleeves = C (3 strands, 4 bullion knots for each sleeve, 8–11 wraps)

Hands and Boots

Hands = A (4 strands, straight stitch)
Boots = G (4 strands, 3 bullion knots for each boot, 8–12 wraps), A (3 strands, French knot, 1 wrap)

Bouquet

Flowers = D, E, F and G (3 strands, French knot, 1 wrap)
Stems = H (2 strands, straight stitch)
Leaves = H (2 strands, detached chain)

MISCELLANEOUS

Juggling clown

This juggling clown is embroidered in a similar manner to the clown with the bouquet. Stitch the hands with horizontal straight stitches rather than vertical ones. Add a tiny thumb in straight stitch to each hand. Work five very loose French knots in a semi-circle around the clown's head for the balls.

Colour

DMC stranded cotton

A = blanc
B = 310 black
C = 321 vy lt garnet
D = 335 rose
E = 792 dk cornflower blue
F = 971 pumpkin
G = 972 deep canary
H = 991 vy dk aquamarine

Embroidery

Head

Mouth = B (1 strand, fly stitch)
Nose = C (2 strands, French knot, 1 wrap)
Eyes = B (1 strand, fly stitch, French knot, 1 wrap)
Face outline = A (1 strand, blanket stitch)
Hair = D (4 strands, French knot, 1 wrap)

Hat

Brim = H (4 strands, bullion knot, 12 wraps)
Crown = H (4 strands, 2 bullion knots, 6–8 wraps)

Trousers

Braces = C (3 strands, 1 bullion knot for each strap, 12 wraps)
Waistband = C (3 strands, 2 bullion knots, 12 wraps)
Left leg = D and H (3 strands, 2 bullion knots, 22 wraps), E and F (3 strands, 2 bullion knots, 26 wraps)
Right leg = E and H (3 strands, 2 bullion knots, 22 wraps), D and F (3 strands, 2 bullion knots, 26 wraps)

Shirt

Front = G (3 strands, 4 bullion knots, 12 wraps)
Sleeves = G (3 strands, 4 bullion knots for each sleeve, 8–11 wraps)

Hands and boots

Hands = A (4 strands, straight stitch)
Boots = C (4 strands, 3 bullion knots for each boot, 8–12 wraps), A (3 strands, French knot, 1 wrap)
Balls = C (5 strands, French knot, 1 wrap)

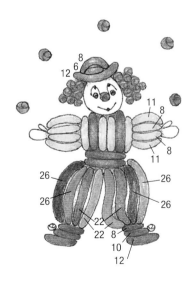

82

MISCELLANEOUS

Birdbath

Beginning at the top of the birdbath, work five horizontal bullion knots following the illustration. Couch each knot in place. Stitch a vertical bullion knot for the stand and then four slightly curved knots for the base. Finish the rim with three long back stitches. Fill in the water with randomly placed straight stitches.

Embroider each blackbird with two bullion knots. Add a French knot for the head and tiny straight stitches for the eye and beak. Finish the birds' wings and tails in straight stitch.

Work the grass next using fly stitch, detached chain and straight stitch, allowing the grass to overlap the base of the birdbath. Stitch the stems of the daisies in back stitch and the petals in detached chain. Finish each flower with a French knot centre.

Colour

DMC stranded cotton
A = 310 black
B = 436 tan
C = 605 vy lt cranberry
D = 676 lt old gold
E = 936 dk avocado green
F = 3053 green-grey
G = 3755 lt sky blue
Anchor stranded cotton
H = 398 vy lt steel grey

Embroidery

Birdbath
Birdbath = H (3 strands, 10 bullion knots, 8–28 wraps; 1 strand, couching; 2 strands, back stitch)
Water = G (1 strand, straight stitch)

Blackbirds
Body = A (2 strands, 2 bullion knots, 4–7 wraps)
Head = A (2 strands, French knot, 2 wraps)
Wings and tail = A (1 strand, straight stitch)
Beak and eye = B (1 strand, straight stitch)
Daisies Petals = C and G (1 strand, detached chain)
Centre = D (1 strand, French knot, 3 wraps)
Stem = F (2 strands, back stitch)
Grass = F (2 strands, fly stitch, straight stitch, detached chain), E (1 strand, straight stitch)

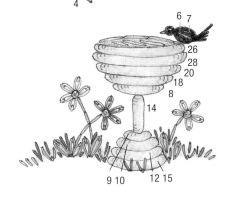

MISCELLANEOUS

Tea set

Embroider the tea pot, working from the base to the top of the lid and changing colour as illustrated. Add a French knot for the knob. Stitch the handle and then the spout. Decorate the pot with flowers.

Embroider the cup and saucer next, stitching the cup from the top down. Add a single bullion knot for the saucer, and finish the saucer with back stitch. Work the lip of the cup and the handle next. Decorate the cup with two petals. Embroider two straight stitches for the tea. Stitch the plate leaving a space for the cup cakes. Start the cakes with the pink icing, working two horizontal bullion knots. Stitch a French knot for the cherries. Work the patty pans in straight stitch, vertical for the sides and horizontal for the base.

Stitch straight stitches for the shadows and steam.

Colour

DMC stranded cotton
A = 311 lt navy blue
B = 451 dk shell grey
C = 828 ultra lt blue
E = 3350 ultra dk dusky rose
F = 3823 ultra lt yellow
Anchor stranded cotton
G = 36 lt rose pink
H = 234 ultra lt steel grey

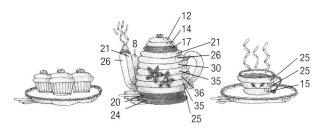

Embroidery

Tea pot
Base = A (2 strands, 2 bullion knots, 20–24 wraps; 1 strand, couching)
Pot = C (2 strands, 7 bullion knots, 21–36 wraps; 1 strand, couching)
Lid = A (2 strands, bullion knot, 17 wraps), C (2 strands, 2 bullion knots, 12–14 wraps)
Knob = A (2 strands, French knot, 3 wraps)
Handle = C (2 strands, bullion knot, 28 wraps, French knot, 2 wraps; 1 strand, couching)
Spout = C (2 strands, 3 bullion knots, 8–26 wraps; 1 strand, couching), A (2 strands, straight stitch)
Flower petals = A (1 strand, detached chain)
Flower centres = H (1 strand, French knot, 2 wraps)

Cup and saucer
Cup = C (2 strands, 3 bullion knots, 15–25 wraps; 1 strand, couching)
Cup handle = A (2 strands, back stitch, French knot, 1 wrap)
Cup lip = A (1 strand, back stitch)
Tea in cup = B (2 strands, straight stitch)
Saucer = C (2 strands, back stitch, bullion knot, 30 wraps; 1 strand, couching), A (1 strand, back stitch)

Plate = C (2 strands, bullion knot, 35 wraps; 1 strand, couching; 2 strands, back stitch), A (1 strand, back stitch)

Cakes
Icing = G (2 strands, 2 bullion knots, 7–9 wraps)

Cherries = E (1 strand, French knot, 2 wraps)
Patty pans = F (1 strand, straight stitch)
Shadows = H (1 strand, straight stitch)
Steam = H (1 strand, back stitch)

MISCELLANEOUS

Noah's Ark

Up to 75 wraps are used in the bullion knots for this design, therefore you may find the extra length of a doll needle helpful. Couch the knots in place as you work.

Start with the housing. Leaving a space for the arched doorway and starting at the centre, work seven vertical bullions on each side. Add a bullion knot for the archway.

Embroider the gable next stitching from the bottom upwards. Stitch two long angled bullion knots on each side for the roof. Finish the roof with a roof cap formed from one bullion knot.

Construct the giraffes next from three shades of felt. Cut out the head and neck shape from one colour and the markings from the remaining two colours. Slip stitch the neck and head in place, followed by the markings. Work a colonial knot eye on each giraffe.

Embroider the hull of the ark starting at the top. Ensure the first bullion knot covers the base of the giraffes' necks. Work down the ark changing colour and forming the shape as you descend. Outline the hull with three bullion knots.

Draw the waves and cloud with water colour pencils. Embroider 6–7 colonial knots around each wave. Above the ark, work eight slanting straight stitches and secure a bead to the lower end of each one for the rain.

MISCELLANEOUS

Colour

DMC stranded cotton

A = 310 black
B = 317 pewter grey
C = 407 mocha
D = 738 vy lt tan
E = 746 off-white
F = 801 dk coffee brown
G = 839 chocolate
H = 842 vy lt beige
I = 3760 wedgewood
J = 3770 lt sand
K = 3773 lt mocha

Anchor Marlitt stranded rayon

L = 1059 lt sky blue

Mill Hill glass seed beads

M = 02022 silver

Embroidery

Ark

Housing = J (6 strands, 14 bullion knots, 8–20 wraps; 1 strand, couching)

Archway = E (6 strands, bullion knot, 25 wraps; 1 strand, couching)

Gable = H (6 strands, 8 bullion knots, 3–35 wraps; 1 strand, couching)

Roof = I (6 strands, 4 bullion knots, 35 wraps; 1 strand, couching)

Roof cap = I (6 strands, bullion knot, 20 wraps; 1 strand, couching)

Hull = C, D, G and K (6 strands, 21 bullion knots, 15–46 wraps; 1 strand, couching)

Hull outline = F (6 strands, 3 bullion knots, 20–75 wraps; 1 strand, couching)

Giraffes

Head and neck = small pieces of felt, B (1 strand, appliqué, slip stitch) *Spots* = B (1 strand, appliqué, slip stitch)

Eyes = A (2 strands, colonial knot)

Waves = L (1 strand, colonial knot)

Rain = B (1 strand, straight stitch), M (beading)

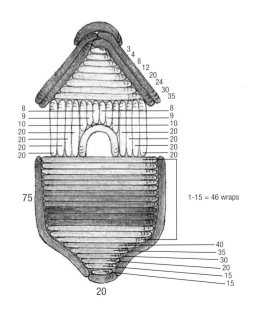

MISCELLANEOUS

Topiary trees

These formal topiary trees are worked using a variety of stitches and are planted in terra cotta pots created with bullion knots.

Embroider the pots first, working each one from the top down. Finish the pots with a small detached chain handle on each side.

Stitch the tree trunks in stem stitch.

Using the dark green thread and detached chain, work the leaves of the left topiary from the outer edge towards the middle. Allow the stitches to overlap. Add pairs of detached chain in the light green thread for highlights. Embroider the leaves on the centre topiary in the same manner, using the light green thread. Stitch the highlights with French knots.

Work the leaves on the tall slender tree with detached chain, randomly varying the angle of the stitches. Scatter French knots over the left half of the tree for highlights.

Colour

DMC stranded cotton
A = 300 vy dk mahogany
B = 301 med mahogany
C = 934 black avocado green
D = 3347 med yellow-green
Anchor stranded cotton
E = 683 ultra dk pistachio green
Madeira stranded silk
F = 1007 med navy

Embroidery

Pots
Pot = A (2 strands, 6 bullion knots, 9–17 wraps)
Handles = B (1 strand, detached chain)

Round tree
Tree top = C (1 strand, detached chain)
Highlights = D (1 strand, detached chain)
Stem = A (2 strands, stem stitch)

Middle tree
Tree tops = D (1 strand, detached chain)
Highlights = C (1 strand, French knot, 1 wrap)
Stem = A (2 strands, stem stitch)

Tall slender tree
Tree top = E (1 strand, detached chain)
Highlights = F (1 strand, French knot, 1 wrap)
Stem = A (2 strands, stem stitch)

NURSERY

Bear in pram

The pram is embroidered before the bear. All bullion knots are couched in place with matching thread.

Pram

Stitch a straight blue bullion knot along the rim of the hood, followed by an adjoining curved blue knot. Beginning next to the curved blue knot, work seven curved yellow bullion knots to complete the hood.

Stitch a long blue horizontal knot across the top of the pram and then a blue curved knot to outline the hand rest. Fill the semi circle formed with two light blue knots and one white knot.

Starting at the top, stitch the remaining yellow bullion knots. Outline the back of the pram with a blue bullion knot, and stitch a small blue knot directly below the lowest yellow knot. Work a long blue bullion knot to outline the front and to form the handle. Add two French knots at the end of the handle.

Bear

Starting at the top, embroider the head. Add two bullion loops, one inside the other, for each ear. Stitch the eyes and nose using straight stitches.

Stitch two bullion loops for the bow loops and two bullion knots directly below for the ties. Use straight stitches to form the bow knot.

Wheels

Secure buttons to the base of the pram for the wheels. Two buttons are used to form each wheel and are attached at the same time.

Colour

DMC stranded cotton
A = blanc
B = 310 black
C = 725 dk golden yellow
D = 791 vy dk cornflower blue
E = 3755 lt sky blue
F = 3772 dk mocha
Anchor stranded cotton
G = 295 golden yellow

Embroidery

Pram
Hood = C (4 strands, 7 bullion knots, 25–50 wraps; 1 strand, couching)
Rim = D (6 strands, bullion knot, 25 wraps; 1 strand, couching)
Rim under hood = D (4 strands, bullion knot, 18 wraps; 1 strand, couching)
Top of base = D (6 strands, bullion knot, 50 wraps; 1 strand, couching)

NURSERY

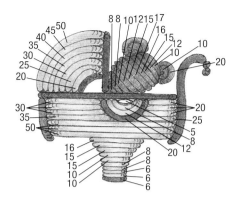

Hand rest = D (4 strands, bullion knot, 20 wraps;
1 strand, couching)
Hand rest filling = E (4 strands, 2 bullion knots,
8–12 wraps; 1 strand, couching), A (4 strands, bullion knot,
5 wraps)
Base = G (4 strands, 20 bullion knots, 6–50 wraps;
1 strand, couching)
Back of pram = D (6 strands, bullion knot, 25 wraps;
1 strand, couching)
Lower edge = D (6 strands, bullion knot, 6 wraps)
Front and handle = D (6 strands, bullion knot, 60 wraps;
1 strand, couching; 4 strands, French knot, 2 wraps)
Wheels = 2 large and 2 small buttons
Bear
Head = F (4 strands, 10 bullion knots, 8–17 wraps;
1 strand, couching)
Ear = F (4 strands, 2 bullion knots, 10–20 wraps;
1 strand, couching)
Eyes and nose = B (2 strands, straight stitch)
Bow
Loops = A (6 strands, 2 bullion loops, 25 wraps)
Ties = A (6 strands, 2 bullion knots, 15 wraps)
Knot = A (6 strands, straight stitch)

Booties

S tart each bootie from the sole and work
towards the top. Add a darker pink
straight stitch across the top of the bootie.
Embroider a straight stitch across the ankle and work a bow
with two detached chains.

Colour

DMC stranded cotton
A = 776 vy lt rose
B = 3823 ultra lt yellow
Anchor stranded cotton
C = 25 vy lt carnation

Embroidery

Bootie = A (2 strands, 6 bullion knots, 6–15 wraps),
C (2 strands, straight stitch)
Bow = B (2 strands, detached chain, straight stitch)

Nappy Pin

E mbroider this quick and easy nappy pin
with two curved bullion knots and fine back
stitch. Couch the knots in place.

Colour

DMC stranded cotton
A = 775 baby blue
Madeira stranded silk
B = 1210 lt Nile green

Embroidery

Head = A (2 strands, 2 bullion knots,
13–22 wraps; 1 strand, couching)
Pin = B (1 strand, back stitch)

NURSERY

Pram

Work this old fashioned pram with bullion knots, starting at the base of the body and working towards the hood. Couch each knot in place to hold the shape, especially on the hood. Work one vertical bullion knot at the edge of the hood and four French knots for the fringe. Stitch the handle and rims of the wheels in back stitch. Add straight stitch spokes inside each rim and a French knot in the centre of the rear wheel.

Colour

DMC stranded cotton
A = 775 baby blue
B = 776 vy lt rose
C = 3823 ultra lt yellow
Madeira stranded silk
D = 1210 lt Nile green

Embroidery

Body = C (2 strands, 5 bullion knots, 15–25 wraps; 1 strand, couching)
Hood = C (2 strands, 3 bullion knots, 8–16 wraps; 1 strand, couching), B (2 strands, bullion knot, 11 wraps)
Fringe = D (2 strands, French knot, 1 wrap)
Handle = D (2 strands, back stitch)
Wheel rims = D (2 strands, back stitch)
Spokes = A (1 strand, straight stitch)
Centre of rear wheel = D (1 strand, French knot, 2 wraps)

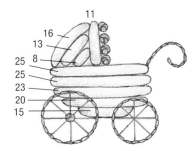

Rattle

Stitch the head of the rattle using bullion knots. Begin with the green knot in the middle and work outwards. Work a green French knot at the top of the rattle and the handle in stem stitch. Embroider the bow loops with detached chain, the ties with back stitch and the bow knot with a bullion knot.

Colour

DMC stranded cotton
A = 775 baby blue
B = 776 vy lt rose
C = 3823 ultra lt yellow
Madeira stranded silk
D = 1210 lt Nile green

Embroidery

Head = B (2 strands, 5 bullion knots, 9–13 wraps), D (2 strands, bullion knot, 14 wraps; 2 strands, French knot, 2 wraps)
Handle = C (2 strands, stem stitch)
Bow
Loops = A (2 strands, detached chain)
Ties = A (2 strands, back stitch)
Knot = A (2 strands, bullion knot, 5 wraps)

NURSERY

Bunny

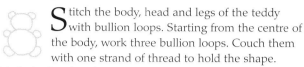

Embroider this beautiful bunny almost entirely with bullion loops. Starting from the centre of the body, work three bullion loops, couching them with one strand of thread to hold the shape. Stitch the head in the same manner, using two bullion loops. Work a bullion loop for each hind leg and for each front leg. Stitch the ears with a detached chain and one straight stitch in the middle.

Finally work the eyes and nose with French knots.

Colour

DMC stranded cotton
A = 775 baby blue
B = 776 vy lt rose
Madeira stranded silk
C = 1210 lt Nile green

Embroidery

Body = A (2 strands, 3 bullion loops, 15–44 wraps;
1 strand, couching)
Head = A (2 strands, 2 bullion loops, 18–26 wraps;
1 strand, couching)
Hind legs = A (2 strands, 2 bullion loops, 15 wraps)
Front legs = A (2 strands, 2 bullion loops, 5 wraps)
Ears = A (1 strand, detached chain),
B (1 strand, straight stitch)
Eyes = C (1 strand, French knot, 2 wraps)
Nose = B (1 strand, French knot, 3 wraps)

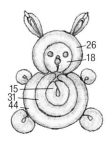

Teddy

Stitch the body, head and legs of the teddy with bullion loops. Starting from the centre of the body, work three bullion loops. Couch them with one strand of thread to hold the shape. Stitch the head in the same manner using two bullion loops. Work a bullion loop for each hind leg and a French knot for each front leg and ear.

Embroider the eyes and nose with French knots.

Colour

DMC stranded cotton
A = 776 vy lt rose
B = 3823 ultra lt yellow
Madeira stranded silk
C = 1210 lt Nile green

Embroidery

Body = A (2 strands, 3 bullion loops, 16–40 wraps;
1 strand, couching)
Head = A (2 strands, 2 bullion loops, 18–26 wraps;
1 strand, couching)
Hind legs = A (2 strands, 2 bullion loops, 15 wraps)
Front legs = A (2 strands, French knot, 5 wraps)
Ears = A (2 strands, French knot, 4 wraps)
Eyes = C (1 strand, French knot, 1 wrap)
Nose = B (1 strand, French knot, 3 wraps)

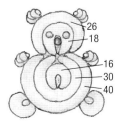

ROSES

Posy with eyelet flowers

Stitch the large rose, beginning with a satin stitched centre and working outwards. Start each round of bullion knots at the base of the flower. Using a dressmaker's awl, pierce the fabric at the centre of every eyelet flower. Embroider the eyelet and then the petals. Work five daisies around the rose, using detached chain for the petals and French knots for the centres. Add the stems and leaves. Finally stitch the white spots in granitos, using 3–4 straight stitches worked into the same holes.

Colour

DMC stranded cotton
A = 3012 med khaki green
B = 3756 lt baby blue
Anchor stranded cotton
C = 976 lt wedgewood
Madeira stranded cotton
D = 0101 ultra lt baby yellow
E = 0111 vy lt golden yellow
F = 0501 ultra lt dusky rose
G = 0502 vy lt dusky rose
H = 0504 med dusky rose
I = 1605 lt olive green
J = 2401 white

Embroidery

Large rose *Centre* = H (2 strands, satin stitch, 3 bullion knots, 16 wraps)
Inner petals = G (2 strands, 5 bullion knots, 16 wraps)
Middle petals = F (2 strands, 7 bullion knots, 16 wraps)
Outer petals = D (2 strands, 14–15 bullion knots, 16 wraps)
Blue eyelet flowers
Centre = C
(2 strands, eyelet)
Petals = B
(2 strands, padded satin stitch)
Yellow eyelet flower
Centre = E
(2 strands, eyelet)
Petals = D
(2 strands, padded satin stitch)
Daisies
Centre = E
(2 strands, French knot, 1 wrap)
Petals = D and E
(2 strands, detached chain)
Foliage
Stems = I
(1 strand, stem stitch)
Leaves = I and A
(2 strands, detached chain)
Scattered spots = J
(2 strands, granitos)

ROSES

Rose sprig

Stitch the full-blown rose working from the centre outwards. Work the rose bud, using bullion knots. Embroider the stems in stem stitch. Stitch the bud calyx and tip in straight stitch. Work the lower right leaf with two bullion knots and a straight stitch at the tip. Stitch the remaining leaves with 2–3 detached chains, placed inside each other.

Colour

Anchor stranded cotton
A = 68 lt wine
B = 859 fern green
C = 860 dk fern green
D = 968 lt tea rose
E = 969 tea rose
F = 970 dk tea rose

Embroidery

Rose
Centre = A
(1 strand, 2 bullion knots, 9–10 wraps)
Inner petals = F
(1 strand, 3 bullion knots, 9–10 wraps)
Middle petals = E
(1 strand, 3 bullion knots, 13–14 wraps)
Outer petals = D
(1 strand, 4 bullion knots, 10–17 wraps)
Rosebud
Inner petals = E
(1 strand, 2 bullion knots, 6–7 wraps)
Outer petals = D
(1 strand, 2 bullion knots, 10 wraps)
Calyx and tip = B
(1 strand, straight stitch)
Stems and leaves *Stems* = C
(1 strand, stem stitch)
Leaves = C
(1 strand, straight stitch, 2 bullion knots, 8 wraps),
B (1 strand, detached chain)

Rose sprigs

Embroider two bullion knots for the inner petals of each rose, and a round of five bullion knots for the outer petals. Stitch two bullion knots side by side for the rosebud petals. Work a closely hugging fly stitch around each bud for the sepals. Stitch the stems in stem stitch and the leaves in detached chain.

Colour

DMC stranded cotton
A = 524 vy lt fern green
B = 950 vy lt mocha
C = 951 sand

Embroidery

Roses
Inner petals = B
(2 strands, 2 bullion knots, 6 wraps)
Outer petals = C
(2 strands, 5 bullion knots, 11 wraps)
Rosebuds
Petals = B
(2 strands, 2 bullion knots, 6 wraps)
Sepals = A
(1 strand, fly stitch)
Stems and leaves
Stems = A
(1 strand, stem stitch)
Leaves = A
(1 strand, detached chain)

ROSES

Single rose 1

Begin with a bullion loop for the centre. Work two rounds of bullion knots for the petals. Add three detached chains to each side of the rose for leaves.

Colour

DMC stranded cotton

A = 316 med antique mauve
B = 524 vy lt fern green
C = 778 vy lt antique mauve
D = 3727 lt antique mauve

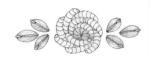

Embroidery

Centre = A (1 strand, bullion loop, 15 wraps)
Inner petals = D (1 strand, 3 bullion knots, 15 wraps)
Outer petals = C (1 strand, 7 bullion knots, 15 wraps)
Leaves = B (2 strands, detached chain)

Single rose 2

This classic grub rose is stitched with three bullion knots in the centre, and two rounds of knots for the petals. Stitch two bullion knots side by side for each leaf.

Colour

DMC stranded cotton

A = 223 lt shell pink
B = 224 vy lt shell pink
C = 225 ultra lt shell pink
D = 3013 lt khaki green

Embroidery

Centre = A (3 strands, 3 bullion knots, 8 wraps)
Inner petals = B (3 strands, 5 bullion knots, 15 wraps)
Outer petals = C (3 strands, 8 bullion knots, 20 wraps)
Leaves = D (2 strands, 2 bullion knots, 5 wraps)

Single rose 3

Work the petals from the centre outwards. Surround the lower half of the rose with a fly stitch for the sepals. Stitch the stem in stem stitch and the leaves in detached chain. Finally, add a French knot bud just to the right of the flower.

Colour

DMC stranded cotton

A = 352 lt coral
B = 564 vy lt jade
C = 712 cream
D = 754 lt peach
E = 948 vy lt peach

Embroidery

Centre = D (2 strands, 2 bullion knots, 6 wraps)
Inner petals = E (2 strands, 2 bullion knots, 10 wraps)
Outer petals = C (2 strands, 2 bullion knots, 12 wraps)
Sepals = B (2 strands, fly stitch)
Stem = B (2 strands, stem stitch)
Leaves = B (2 strands, detached chain)
Tiny bud = A (2 strands, French knot, 2 wraps)

ROSES

Single rose 4

Embroider two bullion knots for the centre. Encircle the centre with three bullion knots for the inner petals. Add four bullion knots to the base of the flower for the outer petals.

Work a long straight stitch for the stem. Add a small couching stitch near the middle to anchor the stitch and distort it into a curve. Using the same thread, stitch four large detached chains near the top of the stem, and two smaller detached chains at the top of the flower.

Colour

DMC stranded cotton
A = 644 med beige-grey
Madeira stranded silk
B = 0815 ultra lt shell pink
C = 1910 lt beige-brown

Embroidery

Rose
Centre = C (2 strands, 2 bullion knots, 6 wraps)
Inner petals = B (2 strands, 3 bullion knots, 10 wraps)
Outer petals = B (2 strands, 4 bullion knots, 10–12 wraps)
Stem = A (1 strand, straight stitch, couching)
Leaves = A (1 strand, detached chain)

Roses and forget-me-nots

Stitch the rose beginning from the centre and working outwards. Embroider four bullion loops for the petals of the forget-me-nots and add a French knot for the centre. Work a rosebud at each end of the design, using two bullion knots. Scatter detached chain leaves and French knot spots among the larger flowers.

Colour

DMC stranded cotton
A = 341 lt blue-violet
B = 503 med blue-green
C = 744 lt yellow
D = 761 lt salmon
E = 818 baby pink
F = 819 lt baby pink

Embroidery

Rose
Centre = D (2 strands, 2 bullion knots, 8 wraps)
Inner petals = E (2 strands, 3 bullion knots, 11 wraps)
Outer petals = F (2 strands, 7 bullion knots, 8 wraps)
Forget-me-nots
Centre = C (2 strands, French knot, 2 wraps)
Petals = A (2 strands, 4 bullion loops, 24 wraps)
Rosebuds
Inner petals = D (2 strands, 2 bullion knots, 8 wraps)
Outer petals = F (2 strands, 2 bullion knots, 8 wraps)
Leaves = B
(2 strands,
detached chain)
Spots = C
(2 strands, French knot, 2 wraps)

ROSES

Rosebud 1

Embroider the centre, making the lower knot slightly longer than the upper one. Add the inner petals directly below, then the outer petals. Work the sepals with two bullion knots and the stem with one knot. Stitch two bullion knots for each leaf.

Colour

DMC stranded cotton
A = 223 lt shell pink
B = 224 vy lt shell pink
C = 225 ultra lt shell pink
D = 3013 lt khaki green

Embroidery

Centre = A (3 strands, 2 bullion knots, 8–10 wraps)
Inner petals = B (3 strands, 2 bullion knots, 12 wraps)
Outer petals = C (3 strands, 3 bullion knots, 15 wraps)
Sepals = D (1 strand, 2 bullion knots, 16 wraps)
Stem = D (1 strand, bullion knot, 20 wraps;
1 strand, couching)
Leaves = D (2 strands, 2 bullion knots, 5 wraps)

Rosebud 2

Stitch the inner petal followed by the outer petals. Starting from the base and stitching towards the bud, embroider the stem in stem stitch. Work two fly stitches to form the sepals. Finally, add a detached chain leaf.

Colour

Madeira stranded silk
A = 0813 lt shell pink
B = 0815 ultra lt shell pink
C = 1510 lt green-grey

Embroidery

Inner petal = A (1 strand, bullion knot, 10 wraps)
Outer petals = B (1 strand, 2 bullion knots, 10 wraps)
Stem = C (1 strand, stem stitch)
Sepals = C (1 strand, fly stitch)
Leaf = C (1 strand, detached chain)

Rosebuds

Embroider two bullion knots for the rosebuds. Add two tiny straight stitches at the tip of each rosebud. Partially surround each rosebud with two fly stitches for the sepals. Work the stems in stem stitch. For each leaf, stitch two bullion knots. Embroider the bow last.

Colour

Au Ver A Soie, Soie D'Alger
A = 3322 pale antique violet
Needle Necessities overdyed floss
B = 142 Grecian olive
Scanfil metallic thread
C = 41730 burnished gold

Embroidery

Rosebuds
Petals = A (1 strand, 2 bullion knots, 10 wraps)
Sepals = B (1 strand, fly stitch)
Tips = B (1 strand, straight stitch)
Stem = B (1 strand, stem stitch)
Leaves = B (1 strand, 2 bullion knots, 5–8 wraps)
Bow
Loops = C (1 strand, detached chain)
Ties = C (1 strand, straight stitch)
Knot = C (1 strand, colonial knot)

ROSES

Posy of roses 1

Colour

DMC stranded cotton

A = blanc
B = 224 vy lt shell pink
C = 225 ultra lt shell pink
D = 712 cream
E = 745 vy lt yellow
F = 819 lt baby pink
G = 3024 vy lt Jacobean green

Embroidery

Ribbon
loops and ties = B
(1 strand, shadow work)
Roses
Centre = F
(1 strand, padded satin stitch)
Petals = F
(1 strand, 5–6 bullion knots, 10 wraps)
Large daisies
Centre = E
(2 strands, French knot, 1 wrap)
Petals = D
(2 strands, granitos)
Rosebuds
Petals = B, C and F
(1 strand, 1–2 bullion knots, 5 wraps)
Sepals = G
(2 strands, detached chain)
White blossom
Petals = A
(1 strand, granitos)
Leaves = G
(1 strand, granitos)

Embroider the shadow work bow loops and ties first. Work the padded satin stitch centres of the roses. Surround with two bullion knots and 3–4 knots. Stitch the daisies next. Work a granitos (using 3–4 straight stitches worked into the same two holes) for each petal and add a French knot in the centre.

Stitch bullion knot bud petals. Work a detached chain on each side of the petals for the sepals.

Scatter leaves among the flowers and encircle the posy with tiny white blossom.

ROSES

Heart of roses

This heart, filled with bullion roses, is edged with running stitch. Start each rose with a bullion loop for the centre. Work detached chain leaves in the spaces between the roses. Fill any remaining spaces with French knots. Embroider running stitch approximately 2mm (¹⁄₁₆") away from the heart.

Colour

Madeira stranded silk
A = 0812 med shell pink
B = 0813 lt shell pink
C = 0815 ultra lt shell pink
D = 1603 lt khaki green

Embroidery

Roses
Centres = A (2 strands, bullion loop, 10 wraps)
Inner petals = B (2 strands, 2–3 bullion knots, 10 wraps)
Outer petals = C (2 strands, 4–5 bullion knots, 10 wraps)
Leaves = D (2 strands, detached chain)
Fill-in dots = B (2 strands, French knot, 1–2 wraps)
Outline = D (1 strand, running stitch)

Posy of roses 2

Line drawing is 85% of actual size

Embroider the ribbon first and then the roses. The stems and leaves are stitched next. Stitch the petals of the daisies and forget-me-nots. Add a French knot centre to each one. Sprinkle pink and white French knots around the posy. Work two circles of scallops and add French knot spots around the outer edge.

Colour

Madeira stranded silk
A = 0812 med shell pink
B = 0813 lt shell pink
C = 0815 ultra lt shell pink
D = 0901 lt blue-violet
E = 1603 lt khaki green
F = 2208 lt old gold
G = 2401 white

ROSES

Embroidery

Roses
Centre = A
(1 strand, bullion loop, 10 wraps)
Inner petals = B
(1 strand, 3 bullion knots, 10 wraps)
Outer petals = C
(1 strand, 5 bullion knots, 10 wraps)

White daisies
Petals = G (1 strand, detached chain)
Centre = E (1 strand, French knot, 2 wraps)

Forget-me-nots
Petals = D (1 strand, French knot, 2 wraps)
Centre = F (1 strand, French knot, 2 wraps)
Stems = E (1 strand, straight stitch, couching) *Leaves* = E
(1 strand, detached chain)
Scattered knots = C and G (1 strand, French knot, 1 wrap)
Ribbon = D (1 strand, satin stitch)

Border
Scallops = G (1 strand, back stitch)
Spots = D (1 strand, French knot, 1 wrap)

Spray of roses 1

Work the fly stitch leaves first. Start each one at the tip and add a smocker's knot at the base. Embroider the bullion roses and buds. Stitch the French knot buds in clusters of two or three.

Colour

DMC stranded cotton
A = 223 lt shell pink
B = 224 vy lt shell pink
C = 738 vy lt tan
D = 739 ultra lt tan
E = 936 dk avocado green
F = 937 med avocado green
G = 3726 dk antique mauve

Embroidery

Roses
Centre = G (3 strands, 2 bullion knots, 6 wraps)
Inner petals = A (3 strands, 3 bullion knots, 10 wraps)
Outer petals = B (3 strands, 5–8 bullion knots, 10 wraps)

Rosebud
Centre = G (3 strands, 2 bullion knots, 6 wraps)*Outer petals* = A and B (3 strands, 1 bullion knot of each colour, 10 wraps)
Calyx = E (2 strands, 3 bullion knots, 6 wraps)
Leaves = E and F (2 strands, fly stitch, smocker's knot)
Stems = F (2 strands, straight stitch)
Cream buds = C and D (2 strands, French knot, 1 wrap)

ROSES

Rose decorated oval

Embroider the bullion roses first, starting each one from the centre and working outwards. Add the bullion rosebuds to the cascade of flowers. Stitch the detached chain leaves and lilac daisies, followed by the cream French knot buds.

The oval medallion is worked from the outer edge towards the centre. Stitch the blanket stitch scallops, followed by a line of chain stitch and then French knots.

Colour

DMC stranded cotton

A = ecru
B = 647 med beaver grey
C = 3042 lt antique violet
D = 3726 dk antique mauve
E = 3727 lt antique mauve

Embroidery

Large roses
Centre = D (1 strand, bullion knot, 7–9 wraps)
Inner petals = E (1 strand, 3 bullion knots, 6 wraps)
Outer petals = E (1 strand, 5 bullion knots, 12–20 wraps)

Small roses
Centre = D (1 strand, bullion knot, 7–9 wraps)
Inner petals = E (1 strand, 3 bullion knots, 6 wraps)
Outer petals = E (1 strand, 3–4 bullion knots, 8–10 wraps)

Part daisies
Petals = C (1 strand, detached chain)

Large rosebuds
Centre = D and E (1 strand, bullion knot, 7–9 wraps)
Petals = E (1 strand, 3 bullion knots, 6–8 wraps)

Small rosebuds
Petals = E (1 strand, 1–2 bullion knots, 6–8 wraps)

Cream buds
Petals = A (2 strands, French knot, 1 wrap)
Leaves = B (1 strand, detached chain)

Oval medallion
Outer scalloped border = A (1 strand, blanket stitch)
Middle oval = A (1 strand, chain stitch)
Inner oval = A (1 strand, French knot, 1 wrap)

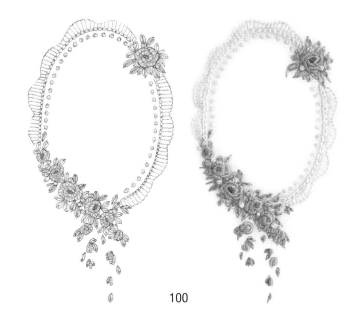

ROSES

Rose decorated heart

Colour

DMC stranded cotton
A = 712 cream
B = 819 lt baby pink
C = 3012 med khaki green
D = 3713 vy lt salmon
E = 3733 dusky rose
F = 3743 vy lt antique violet

E mbroider six segments of shadow work for the heart outline. Stitch a lattice of stem stitch within the heart, working all the lines in one direction before stitching those in the opposite direction.

Work the bullion roses next, beginning each one from the centre and working outwards. Stitch the bullion rosebuds and then the detached chain leaves. The cream and violet French knot buds are stitched last.

Embroidery

Heart
Outline = F (1 strand, shadow work)
Lattice = F (1 strand, stem stitch)
Large side-view roses
Centre = E (2 strands, bullion knot, 4 wraps)
Inner petals = D (2 strands, 3 bullion knots, 7 wraps)
Outer petals = B (2 strands, 4–5 bullion knots, 7 wraps)
Large full rose
Centre = E (2 strands, bullion knot, 4 wraps)
Inner petals = D (2 strands, 2 bullion knots, 6 wraps)
Outer petals = B (2 strands, 6 bullion knots, 7 wraps)
Small roses
Centre = E (2 strands, bullion knot, 4 wraps)
Outer petals = D (2 strands,
3 bullion knots, 4 wraps)
Rosebuds = B (2 strands, 1–2 bullion knots, 4 wraps)
Tiny buds = A and F (2 strands, French knot, 1–2 wraps)
Leaves = C (1 strand, detached chain)

ROSES

Ribbon roses

These glorious pink roses and rosebuds are embroidered with ribbon. Take care to keep the ribbon untwisted and use a looser tension than you would with thread.

Stitch two vertical bullion knots side by side for the centre of each rose. Work 4–5 bullion knots around the lower half of the rose and then 3–4 ribbon stitches for the petals.

Stitch the petals of the rosebuds in the same manner as the centre of the roses. Surround the lower half of each bud with two fly stitches for the sepals and work a single long straight stitch for each stem.

Mingling the two shades of green, work the leaves in ribbon stitch.

Colour

DMC no. 8 perlé cotton
A = 369 vy lt pistachio green
Mokuba no. 1540 embroidery ribbon 3.5mm (⅛") wide
B = 023 vy lt baby pink
C = 034 med dusky rose
D = 356 lt apple green
E = 366 olive green

Embroidery

Centre rose *Centre* = B (2 bullion knots, 4 wraps)
Petals = C (4 bullion knots, 7–10 wraps; ribbon stitch)
Side roses *Centre* = C (2 bullion knots, 4 wraps)
Petals = B (5 bullion knots, 7–10 wraps; ribbon stitch)
Rosebuds
Petals = C (2 bullion knots, 4 wraps)
Sepals = A (1 strand, fly stitch)
Stems and leaves
Stems = A (1 strand, straight stitch)
Dark green leaves = E (ribbon stitch)
Light green leaves = D (ribbon stitch)

ROSES

Rose decorated swag 1

Embroider the roses, followed by the satin stitched bows and ribbons. Work the leaves, individually or in pairs, using detached chains. Stitch the petals of the daisies and forget-me-nots, then add a French knot centre to each one. Finally, add small groups of French knots at the positions indicated on the design.

Colour

Madeira stranded silk

A = 0812 med shell pink
B = 0813 lt shell pink
C = 0815 ultra lt shell pink
D = 0901 lt blue-violet
E = 1408 avocado green
F = 2208 lt old gold
G = 2401 white

Embroidery

Large roses
Centre = A (2 strands, bullion loop, 10 wraps)
Inner petals = B (2 strands, 3 bullion knots, 10 wraps)
Outer petals = C (2 strands, 5 bullion knots, 10 wraps)
Small rose
Centre = A (2 strands, bullion loop, 10 wraps)
Outer petals = B (2 strands, 3 bullion knots, 10 wraps)
Ribbons and bows = D (1 strand, satin stitch)
Leaves = E (1 strand, detached chain)
Forget-me-nots
Petals = D (2 strands, 3–4 French knots, 1 wrap)
Centre = F (2 strands, French knot, 1 wrap)
White daisies
Petals = G (2 strands, detached chain)
Centre = F (2 strands, French knot, 1 wrap)
White spots = G (1 strand, French knot, 1–2 wraps)

ROSES

Spray of roses 2

W ork the padded satin stitch centre of the rose and surround it with six bullion knots for the petals. Stitch the large cream four-petalled flowers next, working a granitos (using 4–5 straight stitches worked into the same two holes) for each petal and adding a French knot to the centre.

Embroider the rosebuds next and add a detached chain on each side of the petals for the sepals. Embroider the leaves and tiny white blossom with granitos.

Colour

DMC stranded cotton
A = blanc
B = 224 vy lt shell pink
C = 225 ultra lt shell pink
D = 712 cream
E = 745 vy lt yellow
F = 819 lt baby pink
G = 3024 vy lt Jacobean green

Embroidery

Rose
Centre = F (1 strand, padded satin stitch)
Petals = F (1 strand, 6 bullion knots, 10 wraps)

Large four-petalled flowers
Centre = E (2 strands, French knot, 1 wrap)
Petals = D (2 strands, granitos)
Rosebuds
Petals = B, C and F (1 strand, 1–2 bullion knots, 5 wraps)
Sepals = G (2 strands, detached chain)
White blossom
Petals = A (1 strand, granitos)
Leaves = G (1 strand, granitos)

Spray of roses 3

E mbroider three bullion knots side by side for the centre of the bullion roses. Work two bullion knots around the upper half of the centre and four bullion knots around the lower half. Embroider the larger rosebuds in a similar manner, using only one bullion knot for the centre. Stitch the smaller pink rosebuds with bullion knots, adding detached chain sepals to the base of each flower. Scatter four cream daisies, with detached chain petals, among the roses. Finally, work individual or pairs of detached chain leaves around the design.

ROSES

Colour

DMC stranded cotton
A = 644 med beige-grey
Rajmahal art. silk
B = 90 winter white
C = 200 barely pink
D = 202 petal pink

Embroidery

Roses
Inner petals = D (2 strands, 3 bullion knots, 7 wraps)
Outer petals = C (2 strands, 6 bullion knots, 10 wraps)
Sepals = A (1 strand, detached chain)
Large rosebuds
Inner petals = D (2 strands, bullion knot, 7 wraps)
Outer petals = C (2 strands, 2–5 bullion knots, 10 wraps)
Sepals = A (1 strand, detached chain)
Small rosebuds
Petals = C (2 strands, 1–3 bullion knots, 7–10 wraps)
Sepals = A (1 strand, detached chain)
Cream daisies
Petals = B (2 strands, detached chain)
Leaves = A (1 strand, detached chain)

Spray of roses 4

Stitch the three large roses followed by the two small roses and the rosebuds. Embroider a fly stitch and two detached chains for the calyxes. Add the detached chain leaves and the French knot buds.

Colour

DMC stranded cotton
A = 3024 vy lt Jacobean green
B = 3743 vy lt antique violet
C = 3770 lt sand
D = 3774 buff

Embroidery

Large roses
Centre = D (2 strands, 2 bullion knots, 6 wraps)
Inner petals = C (2 strands, 3 bullion knots, 10 wraps)
Outer petals = C (2 strands, 2 bullion knots, 14 wraps)
Small roses
Centre = D (2 strands, bullion knot, 6 wraps)
Inner petals = C (2 strands, 3 bullion knots, 10 wraps)
Outer petal on upper rose = C (2 strands, bullion knot, 14 wraps)
Rosebuds
Small buds = C (2 strands, bullion knot, 4 wraps)
Large buds = C (2 strands, 2 bullion knots, 6 wraps)
Calyx = A (1 strand, fly stitch, detached chain)
Leaves = A (1 strand, detached chain)
Mauve buds = B (2 strands, French knot, 2 wraps)

ROSES

Spray of roses 5

Rose

Stitch the bullion rose working from the centre outwards. Surround the inner petals with five bullion knots, then stitch three bullion knots around the lower half of the rose. Add two fly stitches, with very short anchoring stitches, to the base of the rose.

Rosebuds

Stitch the rosebuds at each end, working a bullion loop for the centre and three overlapping bullion knots for the inner and outer petals. Work two fly stitches for the sepals. Ensure the 'arms' of the first fly stitch extend just beyond the tip of the rosebud.

Forget-me-nots

Embroider a complete forget-me-not on the right hand side of the rose, and a partial forget-me-not on the left hand side. Work the petals in granitos using four straight stitches worked into the same two holes. Work a small fly stitch around the tip of each petal. Add a straight stitch along the middle of each petal. At the centre, work a French knot and surround it with a detached chain.

Daisy

Stitch a white daisy below the partial forget-me-not. Work two detached chains, one inside the other, for each of the five petals. Add a French knot for the centre.

Spots and leaves

Embroider a single French knot above and below the large rose. For each leaf, stitch a detached chain with a long anchoring stitch and surround it with a fly stitch.

Colour

Madeira stranded silk
A = 0812 med shell pink
B = 0813 lt shell pink
C = 0815 ultra lt shell pink
D = 0901 lt blue-violet
E = 0902 blue-violet
F = 1603 lt khaki green
G = 2209 med old gold
H = 2401 white

Embroidery

Rose
Centre = A (2 strands, bullion loop, 10 wraps)
Inner petals = B (2 strands, 3 bullion knots, 10 wraps)
Outer petals = C (2 strands, 8 bullion knots, 10 wraps)
Sepals = F (1 strand, fly stitch)
Rosebuds
Centre = A (2 strands, bullion loop, 10 wraps)
Inner petals = B (2 strands, 2 bullion knots, 10 wraps)
Outer petal = C (2 strands, bullion knot, 10 wraps)
Sepals = F (1 strand, fly stitch)
Forget-me-nots
Petals = D (2 strands, granitos)
Petal tips = E (1 strand, fly stitch)
Petal markings = H (1 strand, straight stitch)
Centre = G (2 strands, French knot, 1 wrap), H (2 strands, detached chain)
Daisy *Petals* = H (2 strands, double detached chain)
Centre = G (2 strands, French knot, 1 wrap)
Leaves = F (2 strands, detached chain, fly stitch)
Gold spots = G (2 strands, French knot, 1 wrap)

ROSES

Spray of roses 6

Stitch the bullion roses followed by the petals of the rosebuds. Work 4–5 detached chains for the petals of the blue daisies. Embroider four straight stitches of varying lengths for the stems. Couch the stems into a bunch with two short straight stitches. Add straight stitches to the rosebuds for sepals. Work the leaves with detached chain.

Colour

DMC stranded cotton
A = 819 lt baby pink
B = 3024 vy lt Jacobean green
C = 3747 vy lt blue-violet

Embroidery

Roses
Centre = A (2 strands, 2 bullion knots, 7 wraps)
Petals = A (2 strands, 4–5 bullion knots, 10 wraps)
Rosebuds
Petals = A (2 strands, 2 bullion knots, 5 wraps)
Sepals = B (2 strands, straight stitch)
Blue daisies
Petals = C (2 strands, detached chain)
Stems and leaves
Stems = B (2 strands, straight stitch, couching)
Leaves = B (2 strands, detached chain)

Rose decorated swag 2

Embroider each rose with bullion knots, working two inner petals and then a round of five outer petals. At each end of the swag, work three detached chain leaves followed by three colonial knot buds.

Colour

Madeira stranded silk
A = 0502 baby pink
B = 0504 med dusky rose
C = 1510 lt green-grey

Embroidery

Roses
Inner petals = B (1 strand, 2 bullion knots, 6 wraps)
Outer petals = A (1 strand, 5 bullion knots, 12 wraps)
Foliage
Leaves = C (1 strand, detached chain)
Green buds = C (1 strand, colonial knot)

ROSES

Cottage spray

This elegant spray of cottage garden flowers is stitched with tapestry and crewel wools.

Start in the centre with the large white daisy. Work each of the five petals in straight stitch, starting and finishing each stitch in the same hole. Embroider a fine fly stitch at the tip of each petal. Fill the centre of the daisy with French knots. Add four seed beads over the top of the knots.

Next work the three blue daisies in detached chain stitch. Finish with a French knot centre. Work a pair of blue detached chain petals on each side of the spray.

Embroider the wisteria next, working the stems first. Stitch the large flowers with a detached chain and a fly stitch. Work the two smaller flowers on the longer stems with single detached chains. The unopened flowers are stitched in detached chain using a single strand of crewel wool. Scatter ten pink blossoms around the garden. Each petal is worked with three straight stitches using the same two holes. Work a single French knot at the base of the petals. Outline each blossom with a fly stitch anchored at the French knot.

Embroider five roses, each with a bullion loop centre. Add two bullion knots for the inner petals and two for the outer petals, starting each bullion knot at the base of the rose. Work two long fly stitches for the sepals, ensuring the 'arms' of the inner fly stitch extend beyond the tips of the rose. Add stem stitch stems and detached chain leaves to two of the roses.

Stitch two white daisy buds in the same manner as the white daisy petals. Add the green sepals in fly stitch. Stitch the stem and leaves as for the roses.

Using fly stitch, scatter green leaves and tiny red floating seeds among the flowers.

Line drawing is 85% of actual size

ROSES

Colour

DMC tapestry wool
A = blanc
B = 7020 hyacinth
C = 7028 sky blue
D = 7058 mustard
E = 7196 dk rose
F = 7200 vy lt shell pink
G = 7223 lt shell pink
H = 7384 apple green

Appletons crewel wool
I = 142 lt dull rose pink
J = 209 vy dk flame red
K = 401 vy lt sea green
L = 894 hyacinth

Mill Hill glass seed beads
M = 02019 crystal honey

Embroidery

White Daisy
Petals = A (1 strand, straight stitch)
Tips = I (1 strand, fly stitch)
Centre = D (1 strand, French knot, 1 wrap), M (beading)

Blue Daisies
Petals = C (1 strand, detached chain)
Centre = D (1 strand, French knot, 1 wrap)

Wisteria
Stems = K (1 strand, stem stitch)
Large flowers = B (1 strand, detached chain, fly stitch)
Small flowers = B (1 strand, detached chain)
Unopened flowers = L (1 strand, detached chain)

Pink blossom
Blossom = F (1 strand, straight stitch, French knot, 1 wrap)
Sepals = K (1 strand, fly stitch)

Roses
Centre = E (1 strand, bullion loop, 10 wraps)
Inner petals = G (1 strand, 2 bullion knots, 10 wraps)
Outer petals = F (1 strand, 2 bullion knots, 10 wraps)
Sepals = K (2 strands, fly stitch)
Stems = K (2 strands, stem stitch)
Leaves = K (2 strands, detached chain)

White daisy buds
Petals = A (1 strand, straight stitch)
Tips = I (1 strand, fly stitch)
Sepals = K (2 strands, fly stitch)
Stems = K (2 strands, stem stitch)
Leaves = K (2 strands, detached chain)
Scattered leaves = H (1 strand, fly stitch)
Floating seeds = J (1 strand, fly stitch)

ROSES

Rose decorated scallops

Work seven bullion roses, beginning with the padded satin stitch centres.

Stitch the rosebud petals. Add the sepals in straight stitch and the leaves in granitos (using 3–4 straight stitches worked into the same two holes). Embroider the pink and blue French knots lasts.

Colour

DMC stranded cotton
A = 818 baby pink
B = 3024 vy lt Jacobean green
C = 3747 vy lt blue-violet

Embroidery

Roses
Centre = A (2 strands, padded satin stitch)
Petals = A (2 strands, 6 bullion knots, 8–10 wraps)
Leaves = B (2 strands, granitos)
Rosebuds
Petals = A (2 strands, 2 bullion knots, 6 wraps)
Sepals = B (2 strands, straight stitch)

Spots
Spots on centre scallop = A
(2 strands, French knot, 2 wraps)
Spots on linking scallops = C
(2 strands, French knot, 2 wraps)

ROSES

Spray of roses 7

Embroider the peach rose, followed by the cream rose and rosebuds. Stitch the sepals of the peach rose and buds. Add detached chain leaves along side the cream rose and scatter granitos leaves (using 3–4 straight stitches worked into the same two holes) among the design.

Work the cream daisies in French knots. Begin with the centre and surround it with five knots. Stitch six peach spots around the spray. Work the ribbons in stem stitch.

Colour

DMC stranded cotton
A = 524 vy lt fern green
B = 712 cream
C = 758 vy lt terra cotta
D = 3774 buff

Embroidery

Peach rose
Centre = C (2 strands, bullion loop, 15 wraps)
Inner petals = D (2 strands, 3 bullion knots, 16 wraps)
Outer petals = D (2 strands, 4 bullion knots, 16 wraps)
Sepals = A (2 strands, granitos)
Cream rose
Centre = B (2 strands, padded satin stitch)
Petals = B (2 strands, 5 bullion knots, 10 wraps)
Rosebuds
Petals = D (2 strands, 1–2 bullion knots, 8 wraps)
Sepals = A (2 strands, granitos)
Cream daisies = B (2 strands, French knot, 2 wraps)
Leaves = A (2 strands, detached chain, granitos)
Spots = D (2 strands, granitos)
Ribbons = C (1 strand, stem stitch)

Susan O'Connor

I particularly like to use stranded silk thread for working bullion knots. My favourite Madeira stranded silk colours for roses are 0812, 0813 and 0815 (three pinks), with foliage in 1603 and other flowers in 0901 (blue-violet), 2208 (old gold) and 2401 (white). With one strand of silk thread I use a no.12 hand applique needle, for two strands - a no.10 straw needle, for three strands - a no.7 straw needle, and for four strands - a no. 3 or no.1 straw needle.

When working bullions in wool I like to use a chenille needle, despite the large eye. Wool is slightly elastic and will give enough to enable you to pull the needle through. Thick wool is difficult to thread into a small-eyed needle such as a straw needle. Yarn darners are useful needles for very thick threads.

Many of the difficulties with working bullion knots can be eliminated once you understand how the stitch works. Make a bullion, but before you anchor it, let it go. Trace the path of the thread through the fabric and into the stitch, then back to the needle. This will help you understand exactly what is going on inside the stitch and you will be able to rectify any problems you have more readily.

Experiment with wrapping - clockwise and anti-clockwise. See the difference it makes to your stitches. Wrapping the thread clockwise tends to untwist the thread and makes smoother bullions. Thread wrapped anti-clockwise puts extra twist in, making the bullions tighter.

TRANSPORT

Airship

Start in the centre of the ship with a horizontal bullion knot and couch in place. Surround this knot with two bullion knots and couch. Repeat again, forming the oval shape.

For the propeller, work two detached chains at one end of the ship. Place a straight stitch inside each detached chain.

Work the gondola with one bullion knot couched in place. Stitch tiny straight stitches on the knot for the windows and two straight stitches on each side to form the struts attaching the gondola to the ship.

Colour

DMC stranded cotton
A = ecru
B = 310 black
C = 744 lt yellow
Madeira stranded silk
D = 1802 steel grey

Embroidery

Ship = C
(3 strands, 5 bullion knots, 19–35 wraps; 1 strand, couching)
Propeller = C
(3 strands, detached chain, straight stitch)
Gondola = A
(4 strands, 1 bullion knot, 12 wraps; 1 strand, couching)
Windows = B
(1 strand, straight stitch)
Struts = D
(1 strand, straight stitch)

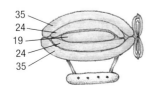

Rocket

Work the rocket almost entirely in bullion knots, couching the knots in position with one strand of matching thread.

Work five vertical bullion knots, starting at the centre. Stitch the nose cone with six bullion knots, gradually decreasing the length as shown on the illustration. Finish the point of the nose cone in satin stitch. Work the base of the rocket with two horizontal bullion knots. Stitch the outer rocket fins with three vertical bullion knots each. The central fin is formed with one bullion knot, beginning between the body and base of the rocket.

Colour

DMC stranded cotton
A = 336 med navy blue
B = 666 bright Christmas red
C = 799 med delft

Embroidery

Body = C (2 strands, 5 bullion knots, 32 wraps; 1 strand, couching)
Nose cone = B (2 strands, satin stitch, 6 bullion knots, 4–16 wraps; 1 strand, couching)
Base = C (2 strands, 2 bullion knots, 14–16 wraps)
Outer fins = A (2 strands, 3 bullion knots for each fin, 10–14 wraps)
Central fin = A (2 strands, bullion knot, 12 wraps)

TRANSPORT

Biplane

Begin stitching this old-fashioned biplane at the engine cowl. Work a bullion loop and couch in place. Stitch the wings in bullion knots next.

Embroider the propeller with a French knot in the centre and straight stitches radiating outwards.

Stitch the wheels with bullion knots and the hubs of the wheels with French knots. Work the wheel struts and wing struts in straight stitch.

Colour

DMC stranded cotton
A = 310 black
B = 321 vy lt garnet
C = 676 lt old gold
Anchor stranded cotton
D = 133 dk royal blue
Madeira stranded silk
E = 1802 steel grey

Embroidery

Engine cowl = D (2 strands, 1 bullion loop, 35 wraps; 1 strand, couching)
Wings = B (4 strands, 3 bullion knots, 16–40 wraps; 1 strand, couching)
Wheels = A (2 strands, 2 bullion knots, 7 wraps), B (2 strands, French knot, 2 wraps)
Wheel struts = C (2 strands, straight stitch)
Propeller = C (2 strands, French knot, 2 wraps), E (1 strand, straight stitch)
Wing struts = A (1 strand, straight stitch)

Yacht

Starting at the base, stitch four horizontal bullion knots for the hull and couch in place. Work a vertical bullion knot for the mast at the centre of the hull. Work the sails from the mast outwards, ensuring all knots are level at the lower edge.

Embroider three tiny straight stitches in a triangle at the top of the mast for the flag.

Colour

DMC stranded cotton
A = 666 bright Christmas red
B = 798 dk delft
C = 820 vy dk royal blue
Anchor stranded cotton
D = 228 emerald
E = 888 golden olive

Embroidery

Hull = C (3 strands, 4 bullion knots, 20–26 wraps; 1 strand, couching)
Mast = E (3 strands, bullion knot, 22 wraps)
Main sail = B (3 strands, 6 bullion knots, 4–18 wraps)
Jib = A (3 strands, 5 bullion knots, 6–14 wraps)
Flag = D (3 strands, 3 straight stitches)

TRANSPORT

Helicopter

Stitch the body of the helicopter, working the horizontal bullion knots first, then the vertical bullion knots.

Work the landing skid with one long horizontal bullion knot, couching in position. Stitch the rotor and propeller with straight stitch and connect the landing skid to the body with straight stitch. Finish by working a French knot on the centre of the rotor, the propeller and the door. Outline the cockpit in back stitch.

Colour

DMC stranded cotton
A = 310 black
B = 321 vy lt garnet
C = 676 lt old gold
Anchor stranded cotton
D = 133 dk royal blue
Madeira stranded silk
E = 1802 steel grey

Embroidery

Body = B (2 strands, 11 bullion knots, 7–30 wraps; 1 strand, couching)
Landing skid = D (4 strands, bullion knot, 30 wraps; 1 strand, couching)
Connecting strut = A (2 strands, straight stitch)
Rotor and propeller = E (1 strand, straight stitch), C (1 strand, French knot, 4 wraps)
Door handle = C (1 strand, French knot, 4 wraps)
Cockpit = A (1 strand, back stitch)

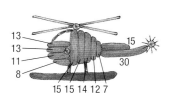

Hot air balloon

Embroider the colourful balloon first. Start at the centre of the balloon and work towards the outer edges, following the illustration for the colour changes. Stitch one small bullion knot across the top. Work the basket with woven filling stitch. Add a bullion knot for the rim.

Work the red ribbons and the lines connecting the balloon to the basket in back stitch.

Stitch a line across the centre of the balloon with back stitch.

Colour

DMC stranded cotton
A = 310 black
B = 321 vy lt garnet
C = 436 tan
D = 721 med orange spice
E = 783 med topaz
F = 3347 med yellow-green
Anchor stranded cotton
G = 133 dk royal blue

Embroidery

Balloon = B (3 strands, 4 bullion knots, 8–21 wraps; 1 strand, couching), F (3 strands, 2 bullion knots, 11–22 wraps; 1 strand, couching), G (3 strands, 2 bullion knots, 11–22 wraps; 1 strand, couching), E (3 strands, 2 bullion knots, 15–30 wraps; 1 strand, couching), D (3 strands, 2 bullion knots, 15–30 wraps; 1 strand, couching)
Basket = C (2 strands, woven filling stitch)
Basket rim = C (2 strands, bullion knot, 13 wraps)
Line = A (1 strand, back stitch)
Ribbons = B (3 strands, back stitch)

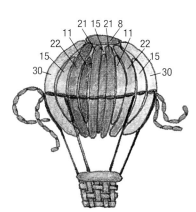

Alphabet

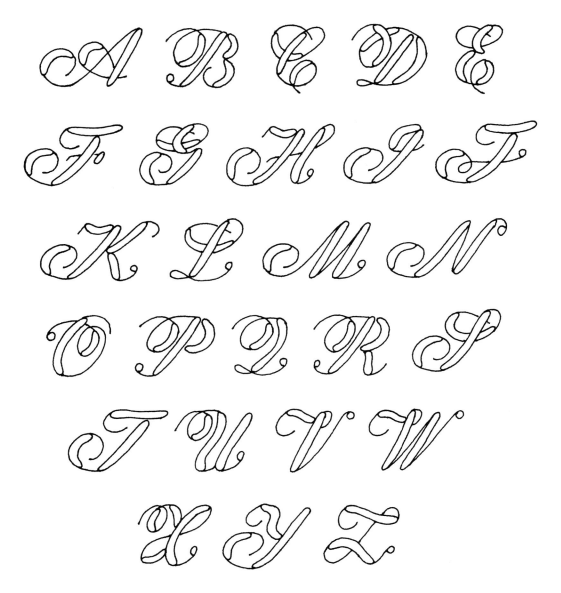

Animals

page 28

page 28

page 29

page 29

page 30

page 31

page 31

page 34

page 34

page 30

page 35

page 35

page 36

page 37

page 38

page 39

page 39

page 32

Australian animals

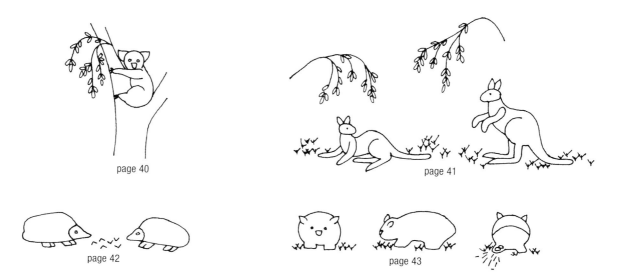

page 40

page 41

page 42

page 43

Christmas

page 45

page 45

page 46

page 46

page 47

page 47

page 48

page 48

page 50

page 50

page 51

page 49

Flowers

page 53

page 53

page 54

page 54

page 59

page 59

page 60

page 60

page 61

page 61

page 62

page 55

page 63

119

Flowers

page 64

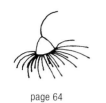

page 64

page 65

page 65

Foods

page 67

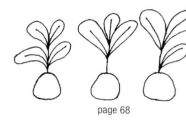

page 68

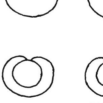

page 68

page 69

page 70

page 71

page 75

page 75

Miscellaneous

page 78

page 78

page 79

page 80

page 80

page 80

page 81

page 82

page 83

page 84

page 85

page 87

Miscellaneous

page 77

page 77

Nursery

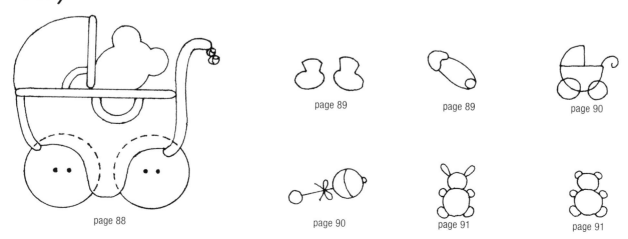

page 88

page 89

page 89

page 90

page 90

page 91

page 91

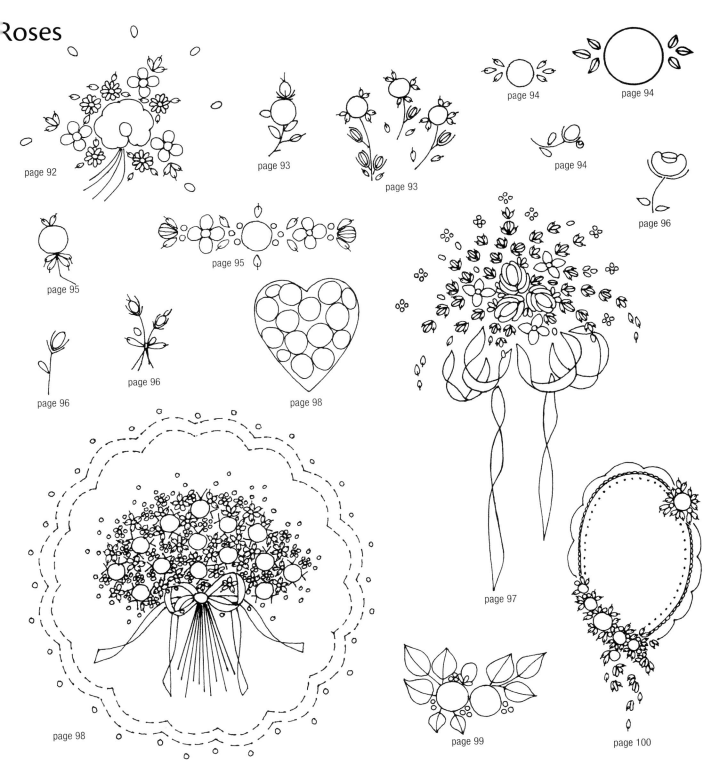

Roses

page 92

page 93

page 93

page 94

page 94

page 94

page 95

page 95

page 96

page 96

page 96

page 98

page 97

page 98

page 99

page 100

Roses

page 101

page 104

page 102

page 103

page 104

page 106

page 105

page 110

page 107

page 107

page 111

page 108

page 113

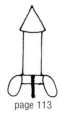

page 113

page 114

page 114

page 115

page 115

Index

A

Acknowledgements 128
Airship 115; *125*
Alphabet 27; *patterns 116*
Animals 28–39; *patterns 117*
Appendix, patterns 116–125
Apples 67; *120*
Aster 59; *119*
Australian animals 40–43;
   patterns 118

B

Bathing huts 79; *121*
Bear in pram 88–89; *122*
Bee 28; *117*
Beehive 29; *117*
Bees, buzzing 28; *117*
Beetroot 68; *120*
Bells 45; *118*
Biplane 116; *125*
Birdbath 83; *121*
Booties 89; *122*
Bottlebrush 53; *119*
Bow 45; *118*
Boy (1–2) 77, 78; *121, 122*
Bucket 80; *125*
Bullion bud on button, step-by-
   step 23
Bullion knot, step-by-step 11
Bullion loop, step-by-step 12
Bunny 91; *122*
Butterfly 30; *117*

C

Cabbages 69; *120*
Candles 46; *118*
Candy Canes 46; *118*
Carrots in a basket 70; *120*
Cat 30; *117*
Cauliflowers 69; *120*
Chalk-based fabric markers 8
Chenille needles 6, 7
Christmas 45–51; *patterns 118*
   Christmas pudding 47; *118*
   Christmas tree (1–2) 48; *118*
Classic bullion rose, step-by-
   step 16–19
Clown with bouquet 81; *121*
Clown, juggling 82; *121*
Cottage spray 108–109; *125*
Couching a bullion knot, step-
   by-step 13
Crewel embroidery needles 6
Crochet cotton 5

D

Daisy, pink 54; *119*
Ducks 31; *121*

E

Echidnas 42; *118*
Embroidery hoops 7
Embroidery ribbon 5
Expert's articles 44, 52, 66, 76,
   112

F

Fabric marking pens 8
Fabrics 7
Father Christmas 49; *118*
Feather 80; *121*
Flannel flower 64; *120*
Flower cart 55–58; *119*
Flowers 53–65; *patterns 119–120*
Foods 67–75; *patterns 120*
Foxglove 59; *119*
Frog, fishing 32–33; *117*
Frogs 29; *117*
Fruits 71–74; *120*

G

Girl 78; *121*
Gum Blossom 64; *120*
Gumnut 53; *119*

H

Heart of roses 98; *123*
Heart, rose decorated 101; *124*
Helicopter 117; *125*
Holly 47; *118*
Hollyhock 60; *119*
Hot air balloon 117; *125*
How to use this section 26

I

Introduction 2

K

Kangaroos 41–42; *118*
Koala 40; *118*

L

Ladybird 34; *117*
Ladybirds and leaves 34; *117*
Lavender (1–2) 61; *119*
Lead pencils 8
**Left handed embroiderers
9** Licorice allsorts 68; *120*
Lion 36; *117*
Little words of wisdom 24–25
**Long bullion knot, step-by-step
15**

M

Metallic thread 5
**Miscellaneous 77–87; *patterns
121–122***
Mouse 39; *121*

N

Nappy pin 89; *122*
Needles 6–7 Noah's Ark 85–86;
121
Nursery 88–91; *patterns 122*

P

Pansy 62; *119*
Patterns 116–125
Peppers 75; *120*
Perlé cotton 4
Polyanthus 54; *119*
Poodles 37; *117*
Posy of roses (1–2) 97, 98–99; *123*
Posy with eyelet flowers 92; *123*
Pram 90; *122*
Pram with bear 88–89; *122*

R

Rabbits 39; *121* Radish 75; *124*
Rattle 90; *126*

Rayon (viscose) thread 5
Reindeer face 50; *118*
Ribbon roses 102; *124*
Robin Red Breast 31; *117*
Rocket 115; *125*
Rose decorated heart 101; *124*
Rose decorated oval 100; *123*
Rose decorated scallops 110; *124*
Rose decorated swag (1–2) 103,
107; *124*
Rose, single (1–4) 94, 95; *123*
Rose sprig 93; *123*
Rose sprigs 93; *123*
**Rose with padded satin stitch
centre, step-by-step 22**
Rosebud (1–2) 96; *123*
Rosebuds 96; *123*
Roses 92–111; *patterns 123–125*
  Roses and forget-me-nots 95;
  123
  Roses, heart 98, 101; *123, 12*
  Roses, posy (1–2) 97, 98–99; *123*
  Roses, ribbon 102; *124*
  Roses, spray (1–7) 99, 104–107,
  111; *123, 123*

S

Scallops, rose decorated 110; *124*
Sharps, needles 6, 7
Sheep (1–2) 35; *117* Silk thread
5 Snowman 51; *118* Spray of
roses (1–7) 99, 104–107, 111; *123,
124*
Squirrel 38; *117*
**Starting and ending, step-by-
step 10**
Step-by-step instructions 10–23
Stranded cotton 4
Straw (milliner's) needles 6, 7

**Susan O'Connor rose, step-by-
step 20–21**
Sunflower 60; *119*
Sunflowers 63; *119*
Swag, rose decorated (1–2) 103,
107; *124*

T

Tacking 8–9
**Tapered bullion knot, step-by-
step 14**
Tea set 84; *121*
Teddy 91; *122*
Threads 4–5
Topiary trees 87; *121*
Transfer papers 9
Transfer pencils 8
Transferring designs 8–9
Transport 113–115; *patterns 125*
Tulip 65; *120*

W

Watering can 80; *121*
Wheat 65; *120*
Wombats 43; *118*
Wool 5 Wreath 50; *118*

Y

Yacht 116; *125*
Yarn darners, needles 6, 7

Note

*Italicised numbers indicate
pattern pages.*

Acknowledgements

Special thanks to the talented contributors who have made this book possible:

Alexandra Baldwin, Kathleen Barac, Robyn Beaver, Barbara Boyce, Jenny Brown, Janelle Buchanan, Jenny Crowe, Sheila Elliott, Joan Gibson, Ros Haq, Margaret Herzfeld, Margaret Hope, Annie Humphris, Marjorie Kavanagh, Denise Little, Gurli Miller, Jo Nowill, Susan O'Connor, Carolyn Pearce, Kris Richards, Jenny Saladine, Beverley Sheldrick, Donna Stevens, Kathryn Trippett, Lesley Turpin-Delport and Fiona Wynne.